To Kimberly !

MW01291749

I dedicate this book to my two children Tanner and Malia. They are my greatest inspirations and examples of love. They will never know how much they have helped me push on through the darkest of nights….

Thoughts become things ! Spread the awakening !!! ☺

Love + Light

Kaji

* Special thanks to Marisa Story Cameron for cover photography, and Trudy Cole for assistance with cover design.

Table Of Contents

Preface

And the living remember those gone
And the gone remember the ones still here
And between the two
A promise is a promise
Across oceans
Across centuries
A circle is completed......
- Kazi Kearse

Standing on the shoreline in Africa, waist deep in the ocean, the welcoming waters splash my thighs. There are many people on this beach, but I am focused on the crashing waves and the slow melodic flow of the tide that I have now become one with. The water speaks to me, and through me. I know that this moment holds right action for me. That it was meant to be so. I know that the difficulty I experienced getting here from America was well worth it.

I am not the least bit cognizant that onlookers might stare at who this strange man is standing in the water, and stretching his arms out. What is he staring at out at sea? Is he performing some strange ceremony? I do not hear any of their thoughts though. I hear only one thought. The call of my ancestors who have waited many lifetimes for me to return here.

I have never felt so at home in a land I had never been to before. At least not in this lifetime.

At the time though, I can remember thinking this was a grand finale to a life long pilgrimage I was making to Africa, my ancestral home. As a biracial African American I grew up around a lot of confusion about who I was. As a boy I was raised by the white, Jewish side of my family, in particular my grandparents on my mother's side. They were very traditional, as was the all white community I grew up in. It led to years of social anxiety, a stuttering problem, and a very introverted personality. Not that I would change a thing, for it helped me learn contrast. Later, in the book we will learn how important contrast is, but for now lets just say it helped make me who I am today.

Some would say I had challenges against me before I even began. I am biracial, and I was born to a white mother, and black father. For reasons that I will get into, I was separated from the black side of my family and raised in a white suburban neighborhood. I'm not sure which came next after that; my stuttering problem, or my social anxiety, or were they both ramifications of my original separation? Love is a powerful thing though, and it lifted me and guided me through the confusion, and dark nights ahead.

I learned the power of love the hard way, through multiple abandonments to follow. Yet from the darkest voids in my young life came a guidance that would grow stronger and stronger in my life. Until on my 19th birthday, when it literally grabbed me and shook me awake!

Looking back now, I hardly remember young Kazi. He seems a mere shell of what I have become. But upon a closer look I realize that he is more like the "core" of who I am now. As time has gone on I have learned to believe in dualities, and I have come to understand this to be one of the many in my life.

See when I began this adventure that became my life, I was completely introverted, yet on the same hand, full of myself, and only myself. I can remember that as a child I use to pretend that I was on my own TV show....FOR DAYS!

What it brought me was a feeling of important unimportance (see what I mean about the dualities). Deep down I knew I was isolated, but I could not summon up the courage, or love, to change. At least not as rapidly as I would have liked. So if I was made to feel like I was alone in the world; I was going to act like I was the only one who was real in the world. Perhaps my broadcast would be seen by some people in the real world back home!

In retrospective, it was my way of adapting to the difficult situation of being raised biracial. Not that I would have changed it for the world. I believe we each choose our incarnations. Mine has been a wonderful one, with a wonderfully select set of lessons.

I was raised by my maternal, white, Jewish grandparents since the age of one. My mother who was 19 and pregnant with my sister at the time, fled with us from my (African American) father, who was trapped in his own hell of substance abuse. We went to live with her parents. Growing up is never easy, but growing up being biracial in the 1970's, in a completely white neighborhood was especially "challenging". The isolation and helplessness only intensified when my mother moved out of the house.

Yet with each tragic blow awaited a blessing, and my grandparents stepped up, loved us, and continued to raise us by themselves. I did not find out till much later in life how redemptive this would be for everybody on a karmic level.

My spirituality was intrinsic, but I didn't have very much actual spiritual knowledge at the beginning and my progress was slow, measured in years, and decades. But like the 100th Monkey, eventually the progress began to be seen in my life faster and faster.

Before I began to journal, each day blended into the other. Sprinkled with occasional victories and insights I somehow managed to eek out a life. Somehow I did not spiral down the slope of isolation I drew into my existence. I did not know it at the time, but I was suffering from Social Anxiety Disorder from birth. In my head all it did was make my show more important.

I had no idea I was being influenced by such forces as heredity, both biologically, and emotionally. I did not know of the struggles in my ancestral line, nor the plan they had for me. A plan that would cross the centuries, the oceans, and the even the grave for me. I could have no idea that one day, on my 19th birthday the hand of God would swoop me up, shattering the existence I had delicately pieced together!

As an adult however, I was drawn to the African American side of my family, and spiritually led by the soul of my deceased

7

father. I had no idea what ancestral forces I would be taking on by traveling to Africa, and completing a circle. I didn't understand the depth of esoteric power that wanted to prevent me from acquiring the spiritual knowledge that I am bringing you in this book, until the engine of my plane caught on fire at takeoff on the trip to Africa! I was undaunted, however, and continued onto Africa where I would visit 3 different shaman who individually gave me the same warning from my deceased father. He said there are forces that are trying to kill me, and had killed him. He said he did not die from the cause listed on his death certificate. I used the shaman's services to repel the attack, and completed the spiritual tasks that day on the beach that I had set out to complete. Flying back from Africa I thought my task was completed. I had no idea that it was just beginning, and that a "new normal" was being energetically prepared for me!

The task of gathering this knowledge of light and dark has been both joyful and arduous. As a young adult I had an unspoken knowledge that writing down my dreams, studying them, along with the fields of psychology, science, and spirituality was meant for something. That "something" however, I could not name.

I combined it with learning about metaphysics. My adventure began freshman year at college when I met my higher self. During a visualization, I took part in at the college one night. I went into an ice cave. I saw a stone figure of a man in a stone chair. He wore a robe and had a staff in his hand. His face was a swirl of rainbow colors. I asked him what is the meaning to life, and as soon as I finished asking the question the reply came, "You"!

He said his name was "Kazi". My birth name is Ken, and that was the name I went by at the time, however I would later begin to use the name of my higher self, as my own first name. So as not to confuse you, I will refer to him as *Kazi* in italics, in this discussion. *Kazi* would later prove to be an import piece of proof for me that another world does in fact exist, outside the physical world I was taught to see as a boy. A few years after meeting him I would see a female shaman named Frauke Rotwein. Shamans are trained to journey to the other side for you, do healings, or provide you with information. She has done all that and more for me over the many years I worked with her. Perhaps the most memorable journey was the first one she did for me. She came back and said she had met a guide of mine on the other side who had a swirl of colors, instead of a face. I knew right then she was talking to *Kazi*, and my world would never be the same!

I would go on to have many spiritual adventures, such as firewalking, sweat lodges with Native Americans, and out of body experiences. My greatest adventure brought me all the way to Africa to do some ancestor spiritual work with local shaman, witnessing spirit trance dancing and voice divinations.

There are forces that didn't want me to complete the work, and tried right from the start to discourage me from the trip. I will explain these forces later in the book, but I had a friend with psychic abilities warn me that dark forces would try and prevent me from arriving in Africa. I didn't fully believe her until my plane's engine caught on fire. As I said earlier though, I got back on the next flight, and continued on to Africa anyway, because I believe it was my destiny to return to Africa and complete a task I was given many lifetimes ago.

Have you lived before? Do you think it odd? It's really not so odd when you think about it. I'm sure you've heard that "matter never dies, it simply changes form". Do you realize that you are made up of matter? They were talking about you. The matter that makes you up was not new when you were born. Even inside the first cell that made you were millions of ancient particles. From many other lifetimes, even cosmic matter from distant galaxies.

Often things are more than they appear to be. I remember when I thought I was nothing before I was born. As if something can come from nothing. Now I know better. Now I know that I am as old as the stars, and that everything is. When I open to it, I can even feel it. When I get real still I can feel the energy flowing through everything. I can even close my eyes and be right there with it.

This book is a guidebook for those who are ready to take an evolutionary step towards actually creating the life they have been wanting. It is not for the "holder-on's" who wish to passively pray that some other entity outside of themselves will save them, or do their dirty work. You will have to pull your own self up. There is tremendous guidance and love waiting to help you in the universe, but make no mistake about it, this is not an easy road. You will have to leave some of your baggage at the wayside.

Sometimes things that were once very dear.

Each person or circumstance we find in our life can be a path for us to self love, or inner happiness. Even the paths that take us down dark roads and end badly for us are also teachers, and were placed on our path for us to grow from. Do you have regrets? Have you learned from them? If you have learned from them can you celebrate the learning?

This book may mess with your ideas of right and wrong, and good, and bad. Hopefully you will begin to see them as continuums, instead of black and white. For the world is not black and white. Look around you. All colors abound! Everything you think you see is really not what it appears to be after all. When you finish this book you will understand that everything is in flux. You, and the world around you are vibrating, dancing, and exchanging gazillions of bits of information with every breath.

Do you think that things around you are solid? They are not! Do you think that you know where you end and another begins? You do not! I will propose to you in the following pages that everything you thought you knew, you now need to look at in a new light. Science is revealing a world far more complex and far more freeing then anyone could ever have imagined!

Just as the world is far more beautiful than you can imagine, I will also show you in these pages that the world is also far more ominous than we are taught to believe! I will offer you proof that the world governments have been corrupted. Not just the small scale local or national corruption of prior periods, but what has now become an international web of corruption, money laundering, and murder. I will not go into extensive detail about any one topic too much in this book. There are other books where you can find that information. The purpose of me providing the information here is to merely wake you up!

There are two forces in this world; light and dark, also called yin and yang. While the force of light grows steadily from generation to generation, progressively increasing its followers, and their enlightenment; there is also a dark force, of people who resist the light. People who seek power and ever increasing monetary gain have erected a web of control, and are devouring each and every one of us in their time.

Do you think this is a conspiracy theory? Well then I suggest you go read The Georgia Guidestones. It's a group of large stones with writing on them. It was put up recently. By who, it is unknown, but it specifically states their intention to wipeout the world's population, down to half a billion people, who will then be sustainable to control. I will outline for you in this book how they plan to go about this. Basically, it has to do with a type of full spectrum dominance, by means of poisoning our immune systems, political corruption, and economic collapse.

I feel it's important to discuss both light and dark knowledge. It is vital today to have an understanding of both. I invite you to google or research anything I say in this book. In fact, I beg you to, because I want you to see for yourself that what I'm saying is really real. Times are such, that if you are not actively working on solutions to the problems you see around you, and actively resisting the dark forces, then you will be contributing to them. Silence is not an option!

The Starfish Story

I came upon a beach where thousands and thousands of starfish had washed up on the shore. I saw an old man walking along picking them up one by one and throwing them one by one back into the sea. I went down and asked the old man what he was doing. He said, "I'm throwing these starfish back into the water, for without the water, they can not breathe and they will die". I said, "But there must be thousands of these starfish here. What makes you think it will make any difference". The old man picked up another starfish, tossed it back into the sea, turned and looked at me and said. "Well my brother you see, it made a difference to that one."

- Darrel Whitewolf

I love this story, and it is so true on many different levels. There are over 7 billion people in the world. A world that has many problems. When I began to awaken I thought that I had to wake everybody else up too. I felt that the entire country, and in fact the world needs to rise up and throw off the oppressors who have been oppressing us for centuries!

As I developed however, I came to realize that not everyone was, nor wanted to, wake up as I did. I began to see that it was not my job to save everyone. Instead my job is to be a source of light, that helps light the way. For me, the way is a way of thinking I call Liberation Psychology.

Liberation Psychology can change not just your political way of looking at the world, but EVERYTHING you know and understand about the world! This book is the culmination of years of research and contains within it's pages everything you need to know in order to think and be free.

Starfish have a special place in my heart. They are creatures who adapt to living in two worlds. There is a time they are in the water, and there is also a time when they are brought by the tides onto the land. Here they enjoy their new normal, and wait for the water to return and take them back out to sea. May this book lift you from darkness, teach you to love what is, till it is time for you to return to the sea, and to love. Like the famous political organizer Harvey Milk once said:

"I want to recruit you"!!!

- Dr. Kazi Kearse PsyD.
August, 2013

Introduction

"You are a den of vipers! I intend to rout you out, and by the eternal God, I will rout you out! If the people only understood the rank injustice of our money and banking system, there would be a revolution before morning."
-President Andrew Jackson

Since the dawn of time there has been an ongoing epic battle between the forces of all that is good, loving, and light; and the dark forces, which feed on fear, avarice and evil in men. I have long since chosen which I would stand with. Being on the side of light my heart is often filled with love and a desire to help others who have lost their way. I know, however, that there is an opposing force out there that works in the shadows, plots, and schemes to gather ever more power and control over others.

The main objective of those on the darkside is power. The main tool of the darkside is money, not just weapons, and land acquisitions. They are only what money purchases them. You will soon see, if you don't already know, that these people have long ago acquired all the money they, or their families would ever need.

Throughout history the wealthiest people have been the people who control the money, originally called "money changers". It was not long before they amassed greater sums of money than even kings and queens.

If they tell you that I committed suicide, do not believe them. I love my life. If I meet some nefarious end, see it for what it was, an assassination. That's how they work. First they try to manipulate you, and if they can't, then they try to kill you. Anything to silence opposition. Anything to maintain their agenda.

I'd be in good company. Many have been done in because they opposed the money changers. Jesus Christ, for example, was crucified only after he threw the money changers out of the town market. Four American presidents where assassinated, but also, only after they challenged the rule of the money changers.

They were Abraham Lincoln, James Garfield, William McKinley, and John F. Kennedy. Abraham Lincoln opposed using the central bank's money, and had begun to print our own American money. The money went into circulation. This must have become intolerable for the international bankers. Lincoln was summarily assassinated. James Garfield, the 20th president, was killed because he opposed the central bank, created by the international bankers, and planed to print our own American money. He only lasted 20 days in office. William McKinley, the 25th president, was killed because he was seeking to create tariffs that would have made the international bankers actually have to compete with American companies. They loathe competition, and so he was assassinated. John F. Kennedy was the darling of the elite, until he decided to stop playing their game. In 1962 he began to take the power to print money away from the Federal Reserve and to print American money from the government. In 1963, he too would be assassinated. Like Lincoln, a bullet to the head!

There have been many other names for money changers over the centuries. I will probably use all of them in this book. Names like, banksters, international bankers, money elite, money trust, oligarchy, and the elite will be some terms I use.

In Part One of this book I will explain who these people are, and how they have come to control every level of society. I will outline for you what they have done, and the lies they have misinformed you with since you were little. It is time that we awaken to the true nature of what they are all about. The awakening will change everything that you thought was true, your understanding of historical reality, and even physical reality!

In Part Two, I will tell you about the true nature of the world you were born into. I will layout for you a modern understanding of the psychological and spiritual laws of the universe and the proper management of thought energy. With this new knowledge you will be able to gain control over your life, despite the actions that banksters make against you.

Part Three of this book describes the plan, and systems you can learn, to take your power back. Eli Wiesel learned a valuable lesson in the concentration camps during the Jewish Holocaust. He learned that no one can make you believe something, unless you let them. That you can be in a ghetto, but the ghetto does not have to be in you!

The international bankers have been plotting, planning, and meeting in secret for many generations. They have the head start on us organizationally, however we have the advantage in numbers, and only need to wake up a critical mass of people to foil their efforts and make a positive agenda the "new normal"!

Part One: How We Became Debt Slaves

Chapter One: The Game You Were Born Into

> " *If the American people ever allow private banks to control the issue of their currency, first by inflation, and then by deflation, the banks and the corporations which grow up around them, will deprive the people of all property, until their children wake up homeless on the continent their fathers conquered.* "
>
> *- Thomas Jefferson*

The Rise of The Banksters

As I stated earlier, there have been money changers, and members of the elite ruling class all through human history. Perhaps no other single family has influenced our modern day economic problem more than the Rothschilds.

Amschel Moses Bauer in 1743 AD opened up a goldsmith shop in Germany and hung an emblem over the door that depicted a roman eagle on a red shield. It became known as the red shield firm or in German, "Rothschild". When his son, Mayer Amschel

Bauer inherited the business he changed his name to Rothschild.

So began centuries of corruption, and deceit, as the Rothschilds figured out that it is more profitable to loan money to kings and governments than to individuals. The loans were bigger than individual loans, and they would be secured by the nation's taxes, which would get funneled to you, the banker.

Mayer Rothschild had 5 sons, and he trained them all, and then spread them out to 5 key cities across Europe. Before long they became the wealthiest family in the world. By financing both sides in conflicts they learned how to profit from war. The also learned that if you controlled the distribution of the nation's money supply you could make unheard of profit from the interest payments you could charge governments. The governments would then tax the citizens to pay for the large interest payments.

The American Revolution was said to have started because the colonies where being unfairly taxed by the British King. This however was only a half truth. The American colonies printed their own money and therefore had no interest to pay to anyone.

The Rothschilds could not let this continue. Through their influence in parliament they had passed the Currency Act of 1764. It ordered them to stop printing their own money and pay taxes to England.

> *" The colonies would gladly have borne the little tax on tea and other matters had it not been that England took away from the colonies their money, which created unemployment and dissatisfaction. The inability of the colonists to get the power to issue their own money, permanently out of the hands of George III and the international bankers, was the prime reason for the Revolutionary War."*
>
> *- Benjamin Franklin*

We are falsely told that we won our independence in 1776. However this is a lie. We may have won the battle, but not the war. The Banksters bought politicians like Alexander Hamilton and pushed through congress the development of a central bank. The profits, and interest payments would still go to them.

One bankster actually defected, and once wrote James Madison, who was working with Thomas Jefferson against Alexander Hamilton and the Rothschilds:

> *" The rich will strive to establish their dominion and enslave the rest. They always did. They always will...They will have the same effect here as elsewhere, if we do not, by (the power of) government, keep them in their proper spheres. "*
>
> *- Gouvernor Morris 1787AD.*

The first major central bank in the United States was called oddly enough, The First Bank of The United States. Like the Bank of England before it, and the Federal Reserve Bank after it, the name was meant to give the illusion that it was a government enterprise.

Through a practice called Fractional Reserve Banking, banks are given the right to make loans on 100% of the money they claim to have, but actually only have a small fraction of it. They then can collect interest payments on the full, imaginary 100% and make truckloads of profits, many times over.

Napoleon Bonaparte opposed the Bank of England, and made a deal with Thomas Jefferson who shared his disdain for the banksters, called the Louisiana Purchase. Napoleon used the profit to finance a war against the Bank of England by way of conquering European countries.

> *" The hand that gives (bankers) is above the hand that takes (government). Money has no motherland; financiers are without patriotism and without decency: their sole object is gain."*
>
> *- Napoleon Bonaparte*

As you know, Napoleon eventually lost. The banksters victory would be short lived though, because here in the United States congress and the American people were increasingly growing tired of a central bank. By a one vote victory James Madison was able to kill the First Bank of the United States.

This really pissed off Nathan Rothschild, who sent a reply that if United States got rid of a central bank, it would meet with a most unwelcomed fate. Sure enough, 5 months after the bank was closed, England attacked the United States and the War of 1812 was on.

I cannot help but notice how the international bankers use the prevailing military power of the day, England, back then, and the United States now, to do it's biding. First they will try to manipulate countries financially / politically. If that does not work than they try to assassinate the leader and bring about regime

25

change that way. Someone more favorable to them. If all that fails then they bring in the most powerful military from whichever country they are using at the time. In 1812, it was England.

The war was a draw. It was designed that way. Their goal was to break the backs of the American leaders who opposed a central bank, and erode their support by dragging them into a long, costly war.. The Rothschilds soon got enough support back in congress to form another central bank. In fact by financing wars and loaning governments money the Rothschilds are said to have acquired half the money in the world by the late 1800's.

Their domination was not always certain as patriots challenged them time and time again. One such patriot was Andrew Jackson who won with a campaign slogan "Jackson And No Banks"! But the victories were always short lived, as the Rothschilds just bought enough politicians to change the laws back. In Jackson's case the banks created a depression and blamed it on Jackson. Soon after that failed, however there was an assassination attempt on Jackson, that also failed, when the gun misfired. The assassin is said to have bragged that powerful people in Europe had put him up to the task, and promised to protect him if he was caught.

Another European that gave the Rothschilds, and the international bankers trouble in the late 1800's was Czar Alexander II of Russia. He ended serfdom with The Emancipation Edict, and led many other reforms.

Czar Alexander II secretly helped Lincoln during the American Civil War. This angered the international bankers to no end! He was a constant thorn in the side of the banksters and after three assassination attempts they finally succeeded in killing him. A group of assassins threw one bomb under his carriage, heavily damaging it, and then when he exited the carriage they threw another bomb at his feet.

Many of the czar's to follow played along with the international bankers, except for one. He was Czar Nicholas II. Nicholas gave parliament, or "Dumas", as they called them, increasing power. He was even beginning to give land to farmers. He had so angered the banksters that they eventually did away with his whole bloodline.

They did this by financing a coup led by Lenin and the Bolsheviks in 1917 removing Czar Nicholas II from the throne and imprisoning him and his entire family in one of their estates. The night of July 17th 1918 at 2:00 am he and his family were awoken by assassins and led down to the basement. In that basement the men, women, and children were all shot and bayoneted till dead!

Nicholas would be the last czar. Not just because they had eliminated the bloodline. Not because they had struck fear once again in the hearts of rulers who would think of opposing them. No, Nicholas was the last czar because there was a whole new system ready to replace him. The Russian Central Bank.

Chapter Two

The Federal Reserve Lie

> *"Those not favorable to the money trust could be squeezed out of business and the people frightened into demanding changes in the banking and currency laws which the Money Trust would frame"*
> - *Representative Charles Lindbergh (R-MN)*
> *(Father of the aviator Charles Lindbergh)*

Jekyll Island

The "Great Depression" of 1929 was not the first big depression that our country ever knew. Around 1907 there was another depression, which some say was caused by "the money trust" in an attempt to scare the people, and bring about another central bank.

After the depression of 1907 the government set up The National Monetary Commission whose "official duty" was to study ways to help this not happen again. However the commission was stacked with people who were favorable to the Money Trust (sounds familiar…aka..Obama's financial reform commission).

The chairman was a well to do senator named Nelson Aldrich, whose daughter would go on to marry John D. Rockefeller Jr.

Senator Aldrich set off on a two year trip to Europe to study their central banks. When he returned he set up a secret meeting in 1910. He called together the wealthiest men in the United States, along with representatives from the big banks. They boarded a train that Aldrich owned and journeyed to a secret island off the coast of Georgia, for 9 days, called Jekyll Island.

One of the participants in later years admitted that it was indeed a secret meeting to design a banking bill that they would push threw congress. Their aim was to stop the spread of independent banks and wealth that was becoming a growing problem for the ruling families. Corporations and independent businessmen actually had enough money in profits that they were financing their own development without needing to borrow money from the big banks and money changers. Something had to be done to stop this. As John D. Rockefeller said "competition is sin"!

The plan however fell apart in congress, as their secret plan became more and more obvious. Aldrich's bill would never see the light of a vote. Instead, the Money Trust withdrew the bill, and began plans on an even more sinister plan B. It was time to buy themselves an American President again. That man would be Woodrow Wilson and after they gave him what they called an "indoctrination course", they were poised to take another stab at installing another central bank into law.

The events that followed would lead right up to your door step today. The banksters are two things, persistent, and consistent. Persistent, because they are often gradualists. Their plans happen over years, and decades. They are extremely wealthy, and do not have to worry about particular deals putting food on their table or not. They are consistent, in that their plots over the ages occur in a similar manner, although the means and conspirators may change with the times. In 1910 a small clandestine group of bankers got together and wrote up banking legislation, which would lead to a new American private central bank called The Federal Reserve Bank. Bankers and politicians met on a private island. It was not covered by the press, but here is a list of who came in secret:

Jeykell Island Participants (Traitors List):

Nelson Aldrich   U.S. Senator
                         Republican Whip in Senate
                         Chairman of The National
                         Monetary Commission.

J.P. Morgan: Most powerful banker in
                         United States
                         (J.P. Morgan Chase
                         Manahattan Bank).

Benjamin Strong   Head of J. P. Morgan Banker's
                         trust Company
                         Would become the first head of
                         the Federal Reserve Bank.

Henry Davidson   Senior partner in J.P. Morgan
                         Company.

Paul Warburg: Represented the Rothschilds
                         One of the world's richest men.

Abraham Andrew   Assistant Secretary of the
                         Treasury.

Frank Vanderlip   President of The City Bank of
                         New York.
                         The largest bank at the time in
                         America.
                         Represented the Rockefellers.

Charles Norton: First National Bank Of New
                         York.
                         Another one of the largest
                         banks of that time.

The Mandrake Mechanism

The Rothschild's and the other money elite have great organizers, and always break spheres of influence into regions. Mayer Rothschild began doing this in the eighteenth century, by sending his 5 sons to 5 different sections of the world to run their banking system; and the Federal Reserve Bank sought to do the same thing in the United States. Thus the Federal Reserve Bank was broken into 12 regional banks, in 12 different regions of the country. The New York Federal Reserve Bank is the most important one, and pretty much runs the policies.

The gears that run the Federal Reserve Bank is a system called Fractional Reserve Banking. The noted political historian G. Edward Griffin called it The Mandrake Mechanism after a famous comic strip magician who could make things appear out of nothing. Basically fractional reserve banking allows the Fed (Federal Reserve Bank), to create 9 fake dollars, for every 1 real dollar it gives a bank. Bank "A" can then loan money to bank "B" and bank "B" can then create a fistful of fake dollars for every one real dollar. This is allowed to proceed up to 30 times, before it has to stop. It's called a Fiat Economy, and is much different from a gold standard economy, that we practiced in the past. It is based on trust that the loans will keep being paid. The problem is that when the economy was crashed in 2008, and the loans stopped being paid, Wall Street banks melted down! I believe that the economy was purposely crashed in 2008, and will explain why later in this book.

Your bank also gets to create fake money each time it gets you or someone to take out a mortgage, or loan of any type. Each loan gets credited to the bank as money it actually will have, even though it didn't have it to begin with. So for example, lets say you takeout a $400,000 mortgage. Your bank is allowed to claim the $400,000 as an asset it now has. Once again, based on the premise that you will pay it back. When you can't pay it back, the bank is in big trouble, because it's already used that $400,000 in loans to other banks, big bonuses, and lord knows what else!

We will never know what the Fed did with all our money, until we are allowed a full and true audit of their books. Since it is part of a web of central banks all around the world, my guess is that the money get's funneled to a world bank and into the pockets of it's owners. The owners are pretty much the same families. The names of the owners is very secret, but it was said that even in the 1800's the Rothschilds had half the money in the world. Today their wealth is estimated between 100 trillion and 500 trillion dollars! Which could make the head of the family, Evelyn Rothschild, by far the richest man in the world, many times over.

It is hard to fathom how one family can own more wealth than most of the nations of the world combined. What is so sad is that they could end poverty in every nation of the world, with just a fraction of their wealth, but instead they only seek ever expanding ways of taking more and more from you.

They were able to amass such fortunes by benefiting from war, often profiting from baiting both sides to fight each other and then collecting on debt the countries ran up defending themselves. They also made profits by getting countries in debt and then charging them ever increasing interest rates.

They are doing it right here, in the United States, with a duplicitous congress that is paid off to standby and watch. The cries of true patriots are ignored, or misdirected by the media, which is owned by the globalists and their minions of corporate media owners.

When 5 men can own 99% of the media, we should know we can no longer get real news.

When the top 1% of the rich in this country own more wealth than 95% of the people, we should know that nothing will be fair. Like a cancer, they devour more and more of what the surrounding healthy cells, in this case people, need.

Money Masters

So how is it that 1% can own more than 95%? How did the rich acquire so much money? Why do the other 95% have so little? It was not through luck, nor an act of God. This inequity is purely man made. In fact it was by design. Thus, what I am saying to you is that the system is designed to fail for you.

The system of Capitalism was preached to the masses, but what was kept from them was the fact that only 1% get in. Just enough to keep the other 99% slaving and producing for the 1%. Quite a diabolically ingenious system of economic tyranny. Economic tyranny that is self maintaining, and can be exported worldwide.

Who is manipulating all this? The money masters have created a giant pyramid scheme. They are at the top. The corporate CEO's and politicians are below them, and are the upper level minions who meet for the elite in public (G20) and private (CFR, Bilderberger) groups, and run the cogs in the machine for them. The next layer are the lower level minions. Each layer is increasingly expandable. The lower level minions are the courts, police, healthcare system, and every other person who is charged with maintaining the status quos, that once again, maintain the power, and lifestyle of the 1%.

You might be in this level? If you are, you need to reexamine your role, and your willingness to continue to maintain the system. For you are no more free than the people you service for the rulers. The paycheck they give you is a shackle. You are scarcely any freer than any slave that ever worked any plantation. At least the plantation slave at the end of the day could fall asleep knowing that they did no harm to anyone.

The final layer, or base of the pyramid are the worker bees. The billions of people who create and consume the products, and funnel the profits up to the 1% at the top of the pyramid. You are seen as highly expendable. The elite at the top of the pyramid call you useless eaters. They will drain you and discard you. There is a whole field of science called Eugenics which is based on finding the best way to stop people who they believe are inferior from reproducing. If you don't believe me type the word into any search engine on the internet.

Whole groups of the elite are into this. The Rockefellers have been funding eugenic organizations for several generations. Deviously disguised as planned parenthood clinics and cancer hospitals. The elite create environmental crises and then also own the means of fixing the crises. A look at the corporate board members will show you that this is true whether we are discussing AIDS in Africa, or flu in America.

By means of a system they developed called Problem – Reaction – Solution. The elite secretly create a problem (blame it on someone else). Then through the media (that they control), they help stimulate a reaction in the masses of people. Then through the government (which they also control), they put into place a solution. Most people will never even realize what was done to them.

Chapter Three

The President Is Not In Charge

" Give me control of a nation's money supply, and I care not who makes the laws".

-Mayer Amschel Bauer (Rothschild) 1792 AD.

I loved my social studies teacher in school! Mr. Schuster always made social studies exciting. Our presidents seemed so gallant. Even in the movies and documentaries I saw they always had one crisis or another to manage. It was clear that the president was the one in charge. There were 3 branches of government. They were set up to balance power, so that no one branch would become corrupt, or over power the others. Everything worked so nicely...

Boy was I sold a bridge to nowhere! Power in the government, is not balanced, and not equal. The president isn't even the one in charge. There have been people, and forces, behind the presidents, that were far more powerful, and whose influence far outlasted any president. In fact when a president became inconvenient or troublesome, they were assassinated by the true rulers. These rulers were the money elite, and their corporate and military henchmen.

There have been 4 American presidents that have been assassinated; not to mention countless number of foreign presidents. It is well known, and admitted to that government assassins from CIA, KGB, MI5, and Mossad, have taken out foreign leaders who their rulers had a problem with. It is only here in the United States that no one will admit to doing the same thing.

Who had a problem with our 4 American presidents who were assassinated? When I researched this particular question I came up with a startling discovery. The same group of people had the same exact problem with each of the presidents just before they were killed. Who was it? Take a wild guess. The central bankers!

I think you will agree if you examine the circumstances surrounding their deaths you will find that each of them had done something to cross the central bankers, just prior to their assassinations. They were Abraham Lincoln, James Garfield, William McKinley, and John F. Kennedy.

We were taught in our history books that the Revolutionary War was fought to free us from control of the British monarch.

This however is only partially true. The real reason was to escape the bankers who used the monarch to enforce ever increasing taxes. Which of course ended up in the pockets of the privately owned Bank of England.

The American colonies printed their own money. The Bank of England could not let this continue and through their influence in the British parliament they had passed the Currency Act of 1764. It ordered the American colonists to stop printing their own money and pay their taxes to England, who in turn pay back their loans to the Bank of England. As we know, taxes go toward interest payments, not for services, and this was true even back then. So the colonists fought to free themselves more from the Rothschilds than King George.

Despite winning the revolutionary war, the colonists were unable to free themselves from the influence of the European elite, who simply paid off American politicians, who in turn did their bidding. One such man was Alexander Hamilton, who helped set up the first central bank in the United States. The early power struggles in the new republic were fierce. Both sides had victories, and a couple of central banks came and went.

Once when the central bank was made to close Nathan Rothschild is said to have said "If the United States got rid of the charter to the central bank it would meet with a most unwelcomed fate". When the charter was not renewed he is quoted as saying "Teach those impudent Americans a lesson, and bring them back to colonial status"! Shortly 5 months later England attacked the United States and the War of 1812 was on! The war was fought until it was a draw, and eventually the Rothschilds got enough support back in congress to form another central bank. When you own half the money in the world it is not hard to get support for your causes. Also, when you loan countries money who are fighting, it's quite profitable. The bankers learned to finance both sides of conflicts, and sit back and rake in the spoils!

Patriots did not give in easily however. President Andrew Jackson was not liked by the European banking elite. In fact his campaign slogan when he ran for office was "Jackson, and no banks"! All through his administration the bankers fought him. They made up lies about him, and funded opposing candidates. He survived it and in 1833 began to take the control of the money supply away from the Rothschilds and the private bankers.

In response the bankers crashed the economy, causing a depression, and then blamed it on Jackson. Jackson, tough as nails, stood up to them and weathered the storm, and won a second election. He eventually became such a thorn in their side that they tried to assassinate him. They tried to shoot him, but both of the assassin's guns miraculously misfired, and the assassination attempt failed. The would be assassin later bragged that "powerful people in Europe had put him up to the task". He said they promised to protect him if he was caught. Jackson himself would later claim that he knew that the Rothschilds were behind the assassination attempt. It is said that there were 5 assassination attempts. He survived them all, however politically the international bankers, where able to buy enough politicians and eventually financed a successful opposition.

The Rothschilds are also linked to a cabal of nefarious men who are linked to arsenic poisonings of 3 presidents in the mid 1800's and to Lincoln's assassination. In a deathbed confession about her father's deathbed confession, the daughter of Samuel Churchill recounted how a man named William Russell, whose family fortunes were made in the opium trade in China, founded a secret society at Yale University linked to the House Of Rothschild. The secret name was Skull And Bones (many future politicians and presidents would come from this secret society).

Through these agents of Skull And Bones and the House of Rothschild, the banksters would attempt to fund the confederacy and create a civil war. The north would need to raise money by coming to these banksters, and the banksters could charge them obscenely high interest rates. It would be a double blessing to the House of Rothschild because a weakened America could not challenge their rule of the world.

The only thing that stood in their way was not being able to control the American presidents consistently. A business partner of Skull And Bone's William Russell, named Caleb Cushing would later be linked to arsenic poisonings of President William Henry Harrison in 1841 and President Zachary Taylor in 1850. A third president, President James Buchanan, was also poisoned by arsenic but survived. Cushing would also later employ a man named Albert Pike to arrange Lincoln's assassination.

Abraham Lincoln ran into trouble with the bankers when he needed to fund the Civil War. The banksters charged him almost 36% interest, and so he began to have the United States government print its own money, at 0% interest. This new United States government money became full legal tender for all private and public debts. Lincoln is quoted to have said "We gave the people of this republic the greatest blessing they have ever had, their own paper money, to pay their debts". It was not long before the money went into circulation, that he was assassinated by a bullet to the head.

There are several interesting, yet alarming little known facts around his assassination. I was taught as a child that Lincoln was killed by a lone gunman. This is false. There were at least 8 co conspirators. Some where hung. Some were imprisoned and some would be pardoned by the next president. Yes that's right, PARDONED!

Albert Pike was among those co conspirators. He was indicted, and then sent to prison, only to be pardoned by the new president. Think the new president felt a little pressure? Another co conspirator named Judah Benjamin fled the country after the war was over. Guess where he went? To England, home of the Rothschilds, to become legal counsel to Queen Victoria.

The United States was not the only country giving the Rothschilds a run for their money. The Czar of Russia, Alexander II was befriended by Lincoln and helped block Europe from intervening in the Civil War on the side of the South. Alexander II was also opposing the Rothschilds efforts in his own country to establish a central bank.

The Rothschild's funded a revolution against Alexander II, and he eventually was removed from power and exiled. Before being removed though he was able to pass several laws that actually gave some power to the people that use to only belong to the monarchy.

For screwing up the civil war (The Rothschild backed South technically lost), and for passing those nasty reforms that were now on the books. Alexander II would be made an example of, even though he was not in power anymore. Assassins were sent to his house in the middle of the night. He and his entire family were rounded up from their beds and dragged down into the basement where each of them, women and children included, were viciously murdered and bludgeoned to death.

James Garfield, the 20th president, was killed because he opposed the central bank, created by the international bankers, and planed to print our own American money. He only lasted 20 days in office. Officially it is said that the lone gunman acted alone, supposedly after a personal vendetta stemming from not getting a political favor. I think that it's much more likely that the entire plot was encouraged by the bankers who were fearful of his presidency.

Garfield was not only a follower of Lincoln, and his monetary policies, but had even gone as far as to make Lincoln's son, secretary of war in his administration. Like our secretary of defense, it was one of the highest offices in the land, and must have made the global elite nervous if not down right angry, since they thought they had settled the matter with the assassination of Lincoln.

William McKinley, the 25th president, was killed because he was seeking to create tariffs that would have made the international bankers actually have to compete with American companies. They loathe competition, and so he was assassinated.

Mckinley was very pro business and a big supporter of laissez – faire capitalism. The problem with that is that the elite do not like to compete with new businesses. John Rockefeller would later proclaim "competition is sin"! Thus Mckinley was aligned on the other side of the bankers.

Following his reelection in 1900 he began to tour the country gathering support for tougher anti trust legislation, which would make it harder for large companies to grow even larger. It was on one of these tours that he was taking part in when he was assassinated. Gunned down by a man with a "European sounding last name", while Mckinely was greeting a line of well wishers. If competition is sin, then increasing competition as McKinely was doing was sinful. He would be one of the few presidents killed, not for wanting to print our own money, but for merely telling the bankers that they could not have it all.

The presidents eventually got the message. Woodrow Wilson would help set up the ground work for the Federal Reserve Bank. He would later go on to write at the end of his life, that this was his greatest regret. The Federal Reserve bank, as outlined in the previous chapter, once seizing control in 1913, began micro managing the economy, and purposely crashing the economy during the depression in 1929 by tightening credit (The same tactic they would use in 2008). There was even an assassination attempt on Franklin Roosevelt, but they missed and shot and killed the Chicago mayor who was near him in the car instead.

Later a more organized plot began to be organized by the wealthy elite called The Business Plot. It is believed that Prescot Bush (grandfather of George Bush) was one of its backers. They would attempt to bring in a former military hero by the name of Smedley Butler who they believed could rally hundreds of thousands of military veterans. Their aim was to either kill President Roosevelt, or at least make him share his power, or retreat from his increasingly progressive and labor friendly policies. Smedley, being the patriot he was, promptly turned in the plot to the authorities.

John F. Kennedy was the darling of the elite, until he decided to stop playing their game. In 1962 he began to take the power to print money away from the Federal Reserve and to print American money from the government. In 1963, he too would be assassinated. Like Lincoln, a bullet to the head.

Another reason why Kennedy had to be killed was his increasing disdain for the Vietnam War. He originally was talked into committing forces, but soon began to question the generals. War is very important to international bankers and the global elite. They profit from the war, not just directly monetarily, but also indirectly by acquiring property, and land use rights.

There are a host of theories on who killed President Kennedy. Some theories have Lee Harvey Oswald as a willing participant, and some have him as a hopeless patsy. All I know is that after he was arrested he said he did not kill the president (unlike David Hinckley who shot Ronald Regan, and, like many, admited it right away). Oswald was assassinated coming out of the police station, before he could talk anymore. Some say that the mafia was involved in both the killing of Oswald, and the killing of Kennedy.

Although they played a part, neither of them had the power to fully pull off the assassination behind the scenes. Only forces inside the government had the power to pull the secret service agents off of riding the back of the car (as they are trained to, and had begun to do, just moments before the shots rang out). Only people inside the government had the power to change the route of the motorcade, as they did. And only a marksman could have fired the last shot that exploded Kennedy's head, which came from in front of Kennedy and to the side. From the grassy noll. The other shots all came from behind the motorcade and were not lethal shots. His brother Bobby Kennedy was also assassinated, when he ran for president, and was going to stop the Vietnam War, but I will keep this chapter about people who were assassinated in the office of president.

There are a lot of questions that linger, like if Oswald worked in the book depository, as they said he did, why would he leave the rifle there? Most assassins who have a plan to sneak in a weapon, have a plan to sneak it out. What was then CIA agent, George Bush Sr. doing in Dallas that day, where Kennedy was shot? Why was the very first thing the new president, Lyndon Johnson, did the next day he took office, was repeal the order for the government to begin printing its own money, and return that power to the Federal Reserve Bank?

All told, there were at least 4 presidents shot and killed, 2 poisoned, and 3 whose assassination attempts failed. That's like almost 1 in 5 presidents, or 20% of the presidents, and these are only the known attacks. All of which benefited a small elite group of families. These families are still operating and influencing presidents today, and do not fool yourself for a minute that the current president is not fully aware of this.

Why is it so important for the Rothschilds and the international banking families to control the president, law makers, and our economy? Is it because their plans are even more sinister than to simply own all the money in the world? Is it also about power? Power to enslave the majority of people into serfdom once again? If this is true, then the last real obstacle for the elite is to remove the United States as a world power. Perhaps we can gain insight from an article published in the London Times, just prior to Lincoln being assassinated:

"If that mischievous financial policy, which had its origin in the North American Republic, should become indurated down to a fixture, then that Government will furnish its own money without cost. It will payoff debts and be without a debt. It will have all the money necessary to carry on its commerce. It will become prosperous beyond precedent and the history of the civilized governments of the world. The brains and the wealth of all countries will go to North America. That government must be destroyed, or it will destroy every monarchy on the globe."

- The Times of London 1862

Chapter Four

The US Government Is In Bankruptcy

" Mr. Speaker, we are now in chapter 11.
Members of Congress are officially presiding over
the greatest reorganization of any bankrupt entity
in history"...
- Congressman James Traficant March 17ᵗʰ 1993

I'm afraid that those words uttered by congressman James

Traficant, back in 1993 were true. In fact this was not the first time

that the United States and its citizens were secretly in official

bankruptcy. It was actually our fourth bankruptcy.

We have been bankrupt right from the start. It's how banks

prefer their patrons, because they can charge them high interest

rates and get away with requiring all sorts of servitude, that they

would never get away with under prosperity. In 1776 we won our

"independence" from England, but we were financially bankrupted

by the costs of the war. We took a loan and entered into a

bankruptcy agreement with the Bank Of England. The terms of this

agreement required us to give our new found property rights over to the bank. Thus the Bank Of England owned the United States Of America.

The Civil War also created another bankruptcy opportunity for the international bankers. The European bankers helped ferment the war, and then cashed in on our weakened state. In return for our solvency they would extract their pound of flesh! They would do this by dismantling the constitution of one of the major countries whose existence challenged the authority of the crown.

Shortly after the Civil War, congress passed The Act of 1871, which threw out our real constitution, replaced it with the corporate constitution, and created the District Of Columbia. The new country would be called THE UNITED STATES (in all capital letters), as opposed to The United States Of America. The Constitution of the united states of America, as it was once written, was changed to THE CONSTITUTION OF THE UNITED STASTES OF AMERICA (a corporate constitution).

The capital letters were placed into the constitution and the name of the country for very specific reasons. The people who drafted the changes where changing the government from a republic to a corporation. In a Republic we each had fixed, sovereign rights, that could not be changed by the majority, or the whims of the powerful. As a corporation however, we now only had "privileges", which would be subject to change by forces outside the individual.

You were also changed to a corporation. Bet you didn't know that! I know, I was shocked when I found out. They don't tell you this in school. However if you look on your birth certificate, drivers license, or any other legal certificate from the government, you will see your name in capital letters. The reason for this is so that the owners of the United States Corporation can own you.

The government does not work for the people. It is beholden to the corporation. The center of the corporation is The District Of Columbia. The lawmakers there work for the corporation, not you and me anymore. The corporation controls the democrats and the republicans. They may try and fool people who do not really understand, but once you know these facts they will no longer be able to fool you.

In 1909 there was a major down turn in the economy (probably purposeful shrinkage of the money supply) and the banksters took advantage again by creating the Federal Reserve Bank in 1913. The foreign owners (hypothecated) were given the right to all land, and all people, inside the United States Of America, as security. In exchange they would issue us credit, and print as much money as we would need. At least that was the plan that was sold to congress. The bank's shareholders (some foreign families) were given title to everything within the United States, and we the people, would be listed as the beneficiaries, by way of a birth certificate. This certificate would be a commodity. Your birth certificate is given specific monetary value and traded on the stock exchange. The red numbers on your birth certificate correspond to your stock number that is traded on the stock exchange.

You didn't know you where traded on the stock exchange? I didn't know either, for the longest time, but it's true. In fact it is estimated that you are worth millions of dollars. You can read more about this in later chapters where I talk about the Freeman and Sovereignty movements.

In 1933, after the banks restricted the money supply, causing the stock market to crash, and the great depression; congress passed The Emergency Banking Act. This dissolved the United States of America, it's sovereign authority, and all of it's governmental bodies. From that day on, the United States Of America would exist in name only.

Authority was turned over to the International Monetary Fund (linked to the Rothschild's). The International Monetary Fund is the "center" of all the central banks around the world. Through similar schemes they have acquired the rights and legal title to most of the property and people around the world.

I find it so sad that politicians have through the ages, sold their countrymen's freedom and prosperity out to the highest bidder. By doing this they have traded our children's lives away in exchange for immediate personal fortune. This was true of colonial politicians, like Alexander Hamilton, and even the Joe Liberman's, Nancy Pelosi's, and Harry Reid's of our day.

While the forces of greed and deceit gather power, and control, there is also a force of change and transformation spreading throughout the world. Part Two of this book will be about how to make that transformation on a personal level. I will share the knowledge, and provide you tools that you can use.

I have developed a system of response called Liberation Psychology. I will layout for you exactly what Liberation Psychology is, and how to use Abundance Thinking to counter act the negative effects of the tyranny dished out by the international bankers. It is based on the two natural states of man, sovereignty and divinity. These will be explained fully in the rest of the book.

Chapter Five

Corporatocracy and Debt Slavery

" Money is the new form of slavery"
- Leo Tolstoy 1900 AD.

Debt Slavery

I want you to forget everything you were taught about history.
Forget who you were taught won wars or lost wars. It is all lies, or
at least so full of lies that it is essentially not trustworthy. You
were taught that America is a government of the people, by the
people, and for the people. However in reality it is a government of
an elite ruling class, in bed with elite large corporations, which are
in bed with a small elite banking class consisting of a few very rich
families. I'm not talking about the billionaires that they parade in
front of you, and have you debate back and forth which one is still
"the richest man in the world". I'm talking about the people who
finance the billionaires. I'm talking about people who have trillions
of dollars, and hundreds of trillions of dollars!

The German Nazi's did not really lose WWII. The elite families, including George Bush's, financed them, and after the war helped them escape and live secretly in other countries, like the United States. The Vietnam War and the Korean War were not fought by America to free anybody, but instead to try and spread our empire and provide beachheads to keep China and Russia in check. One family in particular, the Rothschilds, have had their hands directly in every major war since the American Revolution and have been more influential than the presidents they controlled. By financing both sides of wars elite families have profited from each and every war in the last several hundred years.

Both Iraq wars declared by the Bush family, and the Afghanistan War expanded by President Obama, were also not for freedom, but instead they are a means to secure oil rights, and the production of oil pipelines. If you do not believe me simply read "The Grand Chess Board" by Zbigniew Brzezinski. Like Carl Rove was the mastermind behind George Bush, Brzezinski is the mastermind behind Barack Obama. In his book, Brzezinski outlines why we need to invade middle eastern countries and secure the oil lines.

The money elite use wars to generate wealth. Corruption, greed, and getting something for nothing has been business practice for centuries. They socialize the costs of war amongst the people, and then privatize the profits, to themselves. Until recently slavery has been very profitable for the few owners. However today the people will no longer stand for outright slavery, so the banksters had to come up with a new form of slavery.

Their solution is Debt Slavery. Debt Slavery is practiced on a large scale by the International Monetary Fund (IMF). The IMF is like a world bank. It is the center of the web. Each country's central bank feeds into it. It is a private bank whose owners are secret. Although my readers can guess who is probably behind it. They lend money to other countries, particularly third world countries. Part of the money goes to the government administrators who they have bribed to pass the necessary protections into law. The rest of the money goes to pay increasing debt. The IMF charges the country extremely high interest rates, which they know that the country can't pay back. They then say to the country's government go collect more taxes from the people and give the money to us. Now each person works not to pay taxes for services, but instead to pay back the national debt to the bankers.

The international banking families own both the banks and the corporations that get the contracts that are forced on them to remove the country's debt obligations. So the bankers loan the money, but they are actually, in reality, loaning it to themselves. There is a word for this, it's called Racketeering! They collect interest payments, and taxes, and charge the people for the services. This is the formula that the banksters have used to take over the United States, and every country around the world. Just about all countries now have a central bank, privately owned, and beholden to answering to the world bank, or IMF.

The same formula is used on you on the individual level. Through their large international companies and political ties they cause prices of goods and services, and even taxes, to be so high that the average person must use credit to pay for them. Soon the credit becomes debt as the person slowly finds they are increasingly unable to pay for all these things.

Before they know it, they are a debt slaves. A slave does not need a fence to keep them in at night. For they know that there is no where to run, and they feel that there is no use trying to run anywhere, because the owners have the system all locked up. They are sure that before they could escape their condition, they would be caught, whipped, or worse, and quickly would regret ever running in the first place.

A debt slave cannot stop working. They would lose their home, means of transportation, and eventually their family would be destitute. Thus the fear that they will have no job, can be used by the owners to control debt slaves. It's like the boss man who is forever at watch over the plantation. You don't even need that many boss men. Just a few will do.

The banksters like to cause the debt to keep growing, because the more debt they can tack on to you, the more of your total income they can get you to fork over to them. That is why they were secretly so happy when they successfully caused the stock market to crash in 2008 and they started loaning out all those trillions of dollars. They knew that they would get to collect interest payments on every dollar, several times over!

Every person, whether you live in a third world or western country who pays money to their government through such things as an income tax is a debt slave. The income tax was only developed around WWII. It was sold to us as a way to pay for government expenses, however the government sends it directly to the Federal Reserve Bank to pay the government's debt on the money it is loaning from the Federal Reserve.

Not one penny taken out of your paycheck goes for government services. If you are lucky enough to still have a job, and you receive a paycheck, you are a debt slave! Your money does not go to pave roads, it goes in the pocket of the Rothschilds, and the owners of the central banks.

Your so called income tax is simply an invention of the banksters. The Federal Reserve Bank and the government needed a way for the government to pay the interest on the debt created, back to the Federal Reserve Bank. You were the ones chosen to come up with the money. As our debt increases, so will the amount of things they will need to taxes us on.

So they invent things like Cap And Trade, and Carbon Taxes. These are just tricks to get us to fork over more and more money, that ends up in the pockets of the owners.

The Healthcare Reform Act of 2010 is the same thing. It is a means for the elite to siphon money from the masses to their pockets. The IRS is the collection and enforcement arm of the international bankers who own it. Since they also own many of the large health insurance companies, they "get you coming and going". Meaning that they threaten you so that you pay your premiums to their healthcare insurance companies, and when you don't they fine you through the IRS, and collect money through your paycheck if need be. For the really bad boys, they have the government, it's courts and police ready to arrest you if need be.

What we have in the world now is called Systemic Slavery. It is different from the regular slavery of the past. In this modern form of slavery, people still are paid to work. People are not paid much in this form of slavery, but enough for subsistence living. From that small amount, that the elite give us, much of it is returned through taxes, rents, food, and other living expenses paid to corporations / states. Even money collected by the government through the IRS, eventually trickles up to the elite. The end product of this cycle of money and labor is we build more things for the rich to own. Make no mistake about it, these people will not rest until they have all the money, and all the power!

What Is The Corporatocracy?

The Corporatocracy is a vast interconnected web of people who have been corrupted into believing that this is a finite world of lack, and that if they do not take from others they will have to go without. As a system it is a pyramid, where a few at the top, the owners of the international banks and corporations, control, in a top – down management style, the operations of the minions below them. Each layer, the further down you go, understand less and less of their true role. The only thing that the entire pyramid has in common is the belief about lack, and the dominant role the fear has in their life choices.

At the base of the pyramid are the minions of lawyers, policemen, debt collectors...etc, who are not even anymore aware of the owners than you or I were. They simply share the philosophy that there will not be enough for them and the only way they can have their home, their transportation, and their family is at another's cost. Some may even feel a sense of superiority, or righteousness.

They have accepted Dick Cheney's philosophy that sometimes it is necessary to operate "on the darkside". They have accepted the belief that the world is not inherently safe, and that there are whole groups of people that they and their loved ones, need protection from. They have internalized the notion that "greed is good"! To feel safe they feel justified in dominating, even murdering other human beings. They do not even have to use their own hands, since the state has the means to do that for them.

The Corporatocracy can also be called The Corporate State, which is another word for fascism . Our founding fathers warned us against letting corporations get too much power, however, early on the elite learned how to manipulate the masses of people to act against their own interest. Their tool was fear. Fear that you will not have enough. Fear that your neighbor will have too much. Fear that "those" people will take something from you, hurt you, or somehow harm your loved ones.

Besides selling fear, they also sell envy. If your neighbor has a new car, you must also. If your friend added an extension to their house, you have to too. Certainly your kids deserve a trip to Disneyworld. Their friends went!

The first thing JP Morgan did with his money was buy up all the major newspapers around the country. He didn't do that because he liked newspapers so much. He did that because back then, that was how you communicated with the most people. Today its TV, and Rupert Murdoch and his like, are using the same formula, with the same goal in mind. The owner of a thing shapes its message. What news you will hear about and what you will be influenced to believe about it is shaped by the owners everyday.

They are telling you that corporate personhood is ok. Early in 2010 the supreme court ruled that corporations have the same rights as people to support political representatives and their messages. In a land where the top 1% own more wealth than the bottom 95%, how is that equal protection and representation? No, in fact what it is, is a clear power grab by the Corporatocracy!

911 Was An Inside Job

Throughout history the elite have coalesced power by staging events to scare the populations of a given side, against the other side. The elite learned that you can finance both sides of a war, profit from the build up to war, and the fighting of the war, simply by staging events during peace time to bring the parties back to fighting, or give them ever new enemies to fight, and sources for you to collect money from.

The elite own all the major corporations, so not only do they get countries to loan money from them and thus owe them interest, but the money that the elite supposedly give to the country, just gets put into government contracts with the very corporations who are owned by the people who staged the war!

Corporatocracy is really a subgroup of the Oligarchy. The Oligarchy is made up of the families that own these large corporations and countries. The oligarchs are the ones who are really running the world. They are your true enemy. They like to try and fool you into fighting false enemies, like "the Muslims", or "the communists". All the while they fund those exact people to fight you too.

I submit to you that every event that has led our country into war has been staged by the same elite families; from the sinking of the Lusitania, to the World Trade Center on 9/11. There are many excellent books and videos about the events that took place on September 11th, 2001. I will not try in this book to cover every one of them. I believe, however the following summarizes the highlights of the problems with the official story from the government and the 9/11 Commission. Some of the items in this list you may have heard about, some you may not have. ALL of them have been well researched...

1. The seeds of 9/11 go back to the 1980's - 90's.The World Zionist Organization and the Israeli Likud government of Benjamin Netanyahu, principally Richard Perle, Douglas Feith, and David Wurmser (remember those names). They published a document called: "Clean Break, A New Strategy For Securing The Realm". Which called for cutting off peace talks, launching military assaults on Palestine, and getting rid of Saddam Hussein.

Many of the authors of this document somehow make their way from Israel over to the United States and are given top positions in the US Government. Like Rahm Emanuel, during the Obama administration, they are somehow given "Duel Citizenship" status, and advanced roles in the American government.

- Richard Perle becomes head of The Defense Policy Board.

- Douglas Feith, Under Secretary, Defense Policy Board.

- David Wurmser, Chief Middle East Advisor.

They all help draft the next document I will tell you about.

2. Neo Cons (right wing conservatives) who rose to power under President Reagan, together with Perle, Feith, and Wurmser during the first Bush administration formulate a document and plan called "The Project For A New American Century", also called the PNAC Report. In it they outline that America needs to increase it's military presence around the world, and to preemptively strike other countries before they become too powerful. They particularly mention the middle east. The result will be that America will be able to maintain their dominance and

control of vital resources. Oil is specifically mentioned. The document warns that this will take very long, unless there is a "new pearl harbor".

3. The attack on the world trade center on 9/11/2001 would be used as that "pearl harbor". You may have wondered why George Bush Jr. stood on the top of the deck of that aircraft carrier when the troops had just chased out Saddam Hussein, with the whole war still ahead of him, and pronounced "mission accomplished"? Now you know why. His mission was accomplished! In fact it turns out, that the plans for removing Saddam Hussein where on president Bushes desk on September 10th, 2001.

4. There were many other preparations put in place before the attacks. To get a full understanding you have to look not only at what Al-Qaeda was doing, but also at the above players, now firmly in power in the American government. Sometimes you have to read behind the lines. CIA and Al-Qaeda ties go back many years. Osama Bin Laden was on the CIA payroll for many years, and carried out missions for them against middle east neighbors. In fact it is said that

Al–Qaeda was funded by the CIA and put in place to do two things. To launch operations against American (CIA) enemies, and to act as a boogeyman in the American press, to justify funding the military establishment and the agenda of PNAC. In other words, to act in the interest of the banking families who own the corporations that get the contracts, and loan money to countries. Wars bring countries increasingly into more and more debt.

The CIA tracked (or monitored) each of the so called hijackers before 9/11. One managed to bumble things so badly that he got himself picked up. Yet the real plot was never exposed. The stories of the other 19, mostly Saudi, so called highjackers are very bizarre. I say so called because some of them are still showing up alive and back home in the Middle East walking around. It is said that Israeli Mossaud intelligence stole the 19 highjackers identities. Some of their wallet ids seemed to miraculously survive the incineration of the world trade center collapse and float down for investigators to find during the first few days of the clean up and investigation ? It was also amazing how fast our government had all 19 identities, backgrounds, and photos sent to the news media in really no time at all.

The World Trade Center was always publicly owned. A man named Larry Silverstein, however was somehow given the right to purchase it. Larry is a long time Zionist and billionaire with ties to Israel. He mysteriously worked out a sweetheart deal where he only had to pay a few million dollars for the multiple buildings, and quickly took out several billion dollars worth of insurance on them. Along with the clause that if the buildings were blown up by terrorists he would get twice as much.

Guess who he hired to be in charge of security? President Bush's brother, Marvin Bush. Then weeks before the attack, they decide to shut down the buildings for "renovations". The planners of 9/11 had a problem still. They had the technology since 1984 to remotely fly airplane jetliners into buildings, but the jet fuel, and building materials only burn to a few hundred degrees, however steal, which the buildings were made of, only melts and weakens at several thousand degrees.

An explosive would need to be added, but very few can burn that hot, except for something called Thermite. The debris field at ground zero was full of weapons grade nano thermite. In fact pools of molten metal were found only under the three buildings that collapsed. This is a by product of a nano thermite reaction. A chemical that is only able to be developed in state of the art American military labs. It's not found anywhere else in the world. How was it delivered to The World Trade Center? Remember those renovations? Turns out that nano thermite can be sprayed on, like paint.

There were many manipulations going on, just prior to the buildings being pulled. Pulled means a controlled demolition. Silverstein admitted it when he was being questioned about building #7. He said "that's why we had to pull the building". Then his globalist friends got to him, and a few days later he took his statement back. Seemed he slipped and said too much.

Stocks where being manipulated too. Massively in the days before the attack. As if some people in Wall Street knew that certain companies related to the airline industry was about to take a big hit. Goldman Sachs was not the only ones seeming to have inside information, even companies held by government officials were being sold as if they knew something was coming.

On the day of 9/11 inside information abounded around Washington. George Bush was sent out of town to go read to elementary school children, so that Dick Chaney would have a free hand to manage the events of the day. Chaney had an intimate knowledge of "the darkside" of PNAC and the military industrial complex, going back through several administrations. He needed to be at the helm for those minute by minute decisions. Like keeping those fighter jets far away until they are needed, like the one that shot down flight 93 over Pennsylvania only after the passengers had retaken control of the plane. Records show that Cheney was up early that day and sped to the underground command center.

There were a lot of people that morning who knew something. Someone called congressman and told them not to come in. Someone called over 4,000 Jewish employees and told them to not come in also.

5. Same thing at the Pentagon. The "so called" plane only hit the side of the building that was under renovation. Conveniently, Rumsfeld and crew were clear on the other side of the building. It's very mysterious how with all the video cameras around the highest security building in the world, they will only show us one blurry image of something white hitting the building.

    Private businesses in the area had video footage, but the government came and took it from them, and never returned any of it. Same thing with all the audio tape from the cock pit black boxes. Some they kept, some they ripped up. No reason given, and no disciplining of the people who shredded it.

It does not even seem likely that a plane hit the Pentagon at all. The plane, particularly the engines, were never found in the building. In fact the hole that was originally made in the building was too small for it to have been the commercial airliner that they say it was. Experienced pilots have said that THEY even could not even have flown into the pentagon the way they claimed this plane did.

They also point to the fact that there is no ground dug up in front of the building, which surely would have happened if a plane that size was coming in from a banked turn at a high rate of speed. Nothing, that is not computer guided, could have hit the building with such precision. Certainly not a first time amateur pilot.

6. Problem – Reaction – Solution: The attack on the world trade center, put together by the Neo Cons and the former Israeli Likud Zionists, would be very profitable for them and their financial masters, the international banking families, because remember how the elite make money; by selling wars. The problem: "Terrorism", gets sold to the American people through the media machine the elite own. The reaction, is that we willingly give up our freedoms for a (false) sense of security. The solution, authoritarian control, that then can be incrementally stepped up to tyranny…"full control"…Full Spectrum Dominance by a small elite…and

the whole world will be swallowed up in it before they can do anything about it!

7. Once they control everything they can turn up the tyranny. They can collapse economies and get us to work more and more for them. They can poison us. They can imprison us. All without trial. For they are now, judge (regulators), jury (press) and executioner (law enforcement). Their minion's often cycle around and back again, from jobs in the corporate world, to jobs as lobbyists, to jobs as government regulators, then back again to the corporate world....etc.

Merger of Corporation + State = Fascism

It may be hard to fathom, but I can remember since I was a kid, hearing that big brother was coming. In school we had to read George Orwell's book 1984. We would debate whether it would really happen, and as the year 1984 came and went, I can remember being relieved that everything seemed still the same. It was the 1980's and except for some laid off air line workers, everything seemed fine. It seemed that the totalitarian threat forecasted was false. Boy were we ever snookered!

The violent government clampdown we all where watching for never materialized. Instead a soft, friendly form of fascism was snuck in it's place. This new form of government does not require a Gestapo ordering you around at gunpoint. It's much more subtle, and it's made up of people we know around us, like the neighbor down the street, reporting the size of your garden, or the telephone operator secretly working for the NSA. Maybe even your friend on Facebook is spying or informing on you?

It is estimated that the security state now partners with some 800,000 civilians. Just like you and me. Most, voluntarily. Some believe they are helping keep America safe from various threats like terrorists or illegal immigrants…etc. Some just do it to feel important. I would call it identifying with the oppressor, but we won't get into the psychology of it right now.

The following is from an essay by Steven Yates and based on the work of Joan Veon who used the term "Soft Fascism" and Bertram Gross who called it "Friendly Fascism" to explain the system of control that began in the 1940's and is taking fruit in front of our very eyes, today:

A public-private partnership will always have as its goal a business-making venture that requires some form of "governance." The question is, since the players will vary in experience and wealth, who has the most power? We know from life itself that whoever has the most money has the power. For example, when a public-private partnership is comprised of governments such as the County Department of Environmental Initiatives, the State Department of Environmental Resources; a number of private entities such as a land trust (foundation) and the Nature Conservancy (nonprofit); along with a corporation such as Black and Decker, the players with the most money control the partnership. In this case, it would be the Nature Conservancy with assets of over 12.1 billion, and Black and Decker Corporation with a capitalization of $1.6billion.

Representative government loses. By this method, then, citizens are deprived of private property rights and control over their lives and business activities. When private companies must compete in an open market for the best employees and for customers, that is free enterprise capitalism (or laissez-faire). However, when they form partnerships with government, or when either one "partners" with foundations or nonprofit sector entities, or even, I would argue, are legally able to borrow money from banks created according to the fractional reserve system, free enterprise is compromised.

The economic system begins its move from a one based on liberty and productivity to one based on control and plunder. If corporations have the most money—as is often the case—they will obtain levels of power that make them as dangerous as any government not on a constitutional leash. Fascism is the name we give to the ideology which merges the power of the purse(business, foundations, nonprofits) with the power of the sword (government) in order to create policy, impose it by methods ranging from subterfuge to force, and take a society in a desired direction. Webster's New Collegiate Dictionary defines fascism as "a political philosophy, movement, or regime that exalts nation and often race above the individual and that stands for a centralized, autocratic government headed by a dictatorial leader, severe economic and social regimentation, and forcible suppression of opposition." Perhaps still better:

Although the classic fascists openly subverted constitutional democracy, they took great pains to conceal the Big Capital-Big Government partnership. One device for doing this was the myth of "corporatism" or the "corporate state." In place of geographically elected parliaments, the Italians and the Germans set up elaborate systems whereby every interest in the country— including labor—was to be "functionally represented." In fact, the main function was to provide facades behind which the decisions were made by intricate networks of business cartels working closely with military officers and their own people in civilian government. Today's public-private partnerships have these same ingredients even if the main power players have changed. The process of "reinventing government" that took the country by storm during the Clinton years is the best means of understanding the political environment in which public-private partnerships are most at home.

American history discloses two broad philosophies of education, what I will call the classical model and the vocational model. The classical model incorporates the full scope of liberal arts, including history and civics, logic and philosophy, theology, mathematics as reasoning, economics including personal finance and money management. Its goal is an informed citizen who understands something of his or her heritage and of the principles of sound government and sound economics generally. The vocational model considers education sufficient if it enables the graduate to be a tradesman or obedient worker. History, logic, etc., have little to contribute to this, and so are ratcheted down, as in the School-To-Work models. Mathematical education, for example, will be sufficient if it enables students to use calculators instead of their brains. Government schools, over recent decades, have been increasingly bent in the direction of the vocational model. This is known colloquially as "dumbing down".

The result of this process is a graduate who will follow his leaders, be they governmental or corporate, directly into public-private partnerships because, having no knowledge of their problems both economic and constitutional, he has no other points of reference. In our situation, vocational programs "school" students to fit the needs of the "global economy" seen as an autonomous, collective endeavor, instead of educating individuals to find their own ways in the world, shaping the economy to meet their needs. This system is fascist since it involves corporations and governments working together to make policy; it is soft fascist because (due to the lack of genuine education) it is not overtly totalitarian.

Tyrannical controls are barely needed, because among the mind controlled workers and future workers there is little resistance. Most go along, fearing unemployment. After all, as George Orwell once observed, "Circus dogs jump when the trainer cracks his whip, but the really well-trained dog is the one that turns his somersault when there is no whip." Soft fascism thus employs behavior modification rather than obvious acts of tyranny. It is guided by an incentive system rather than overt acts of coercion Thus for much of the population, there is no whip. Those who do not turn their somersaults—perhaps out of a realization that their choices have been artificially reduced—are marginalized and eventually able to find only menial jobs.

Goals:

(1) Global economics, built up as managed-capitalism in order to exploit the enormous wealth available through corporations of all sizes, especially multinational and transnational;

(2) Global government seen as necessary to regulate trade within this global economy, also built up through progressive regionalization, as "the end run around national sovereignty, eroding it piece by piece".

Achieving (1) means (for example): appearing to advance global free trade while actually destroying private property rights, existing prosperity, and government by consent of the governed. It has involved employing pseudo-free trade agreements (e.g.,NAFTA, CAFTA, FTAA, etc.) and other devices where necessary (e.g., SPP) to bring about a migration of power to transnational organizations such as the UN, GATT, the WTO, the Bank for International Settlements and the World Economic Forum, among others. It is important to realize, with a nod to

Orwell, that in the contemporary setting, "free trade" no more means free trade than freedom means slavery. They will however allow "pockets" of economic free choice if they serve special purposes, such as locally owned small businesses being forced to close when people choose to shop at the newly opened Wal-Mart.

Achieving (2) calls for the erosion and eventual elimination of national sovereignty, a natural outcome of the processes just sketched. The gradualist regionalization process was championed by Zbigniew Brzezinski in his book Between Two Ages. This book laid out the entire agenda that has been pursued under the Orwellian "free trade" rubric in the chapter entitled "The Third American Revolution." Gradualist regionalization was again championed at Mikhail Gorbachev's first State of the World Forum in 1995.Arguably it has been almost achieved under the auspices of the European Union, and its advocates in our hemisphere are using the EU as a model to create a "North American Union."

Progress on the first two areas began at least in the 1940s, which saw both the creation of the UN and GATT; it began to pick up speed in the 1970s following the publication of Brzezenski's book and David Rockefeller's creation of the Trilateral Commission. The1980s saw the creation of enterprise zones, under the realization that carefully managed capitalism would more easily evolve into a workable global socialism than the "actually existing socialism" in places such as the Soviet Union, the collapse of which was engineered under the watchful eye of globalist Mikhail Gorbachev. In the 1990s, with NAFTA and the WTO, this agenda accelerated rapidly, and has continued to the point where it can be argued that we have, in fact, sacrificed a substantial fraction of our national sovereignty as well as seen much of our middle class destroyed.

Public-private partnerships are a key component of this overall process. They invariably involve "governance," working under the assumption not merely that government cannot get the job done but that freedom cannot get it done. In so doing, they effectively merge large business and large governments in ways characteristic of fascism. Combined with education that stresses vocation at the expense of subjects such as history, logic, personal *finance, comparative economic systems, etc., they lead to the rise of home grown soft fascism with which an unthinking mass will readily comply. Ultimately, this system threatens Americans with the equivalent of totalitarian controls— as those who stop their somersaults, will lead to the coming of the whips.*

The globalist plan for the world will, of course, eventually fail; the economics it requires (of massive borrowing and theft through redistribution of the world's resources) is out of accord with the requirements reality places on us if we are to achieve genuine freedom and lasting prosperity. It will not fail immediately, however, and if allowed to run its course will wreak havoc across the entire globe, after having destroyed the one civilization that gave the globe ideals of liberty worth emulating. Exposing the growing edifice of controls on individual freedom contained within sustainable development through public-private partnerships is necessary if we are to get rid of this hidden threat to liberty in our lifetimes, and begin the job of restoring individual liberty and private property rights.

PART TWO
Principles Of Liberation Psychology
Chapter Six
The Great Global Awakening

"Welcome to the Great Global Awakening! Much like the old Age of Enlightenment it is a time of a mass change in consciousness. A fundamental new understanding of who man is and where he is from. Old ways are being replaced by radically new, and advanced technologies. Our understanding of science, politics, and religion are transforming into a singularity that will be understood as ENERGY. Energy Dynamics will be used to explain not only the physical sciences, but also the social sciences. It will also be used to explain religion and religious experiences, that will now be accessible to every human. This new age will develop not just a renaissance man and woman, but a completely enlightened universal being".

~ Kazi Kearse

The New Core Beliefs:

Thoughts Become Things- This is meant to be understood literally. The # 1 rule in the universe is the Law of Attraction, which states that like is attracted to like. It holds true whether you are talking about people in social situations, or great cosmic forces. That which is likened to itself is drawn. Thus the frequency of our thought attracts other frequencies of thoughts to it, which are of a similar vibration.

This action causes thoughts to become repetitive, and make our emotions spiral downward, or upward. Take for example someone named John, who wakes up on Monday and his first thought of the day is I hate going into work on Mondays....Then I hate my job....The week is so long....etc. His negative thoughts grow more and more. Gradually his brain changes its chemical outputs. His mind is flooded with chemicals that bring his mood down further still.

He should not be surprised if he trips going down his stoop, or finds another way to subconsciously not even make it in to work, like getting into an accident, even while parked at the light. His thoughts have become things! Thoughts become frequencies, which become chemicals, which become emotions, which influence our choices and affect our physical world. But remember you aren't the only one emitting frequencies. So is every other single thing around you. Your husband, your child, your dog, the trees, your car, the co worker next to you....etc. The list is endless.

The good news is that the opposite is also true. Positive thoughts are equally, if not more attractable. John could choose to think positive thoughts when rising out of bed. Gradually his brain will output all it's feel good chemicals. His mood spirals up all day. People are glad to see him. Good things happen to him when he arrives at work. He is even given the assignment he's been hoping for!

Now I recognize that this is an over simplification. Our days are usually not all good or all bad. For most of us we cycle up and down. However, the point is that when we consciously choose higher frequency thoughts (good thoughts), we bring more positive things into our reality.

The teachings of Abraham offer a wonderful framework to use to move along the 12 steps that I will soon outline to manifest your desires. Esther Hicks works with a collective of entities that she channels who call themselves Abraham. Abraham teaches how to manifest your desires by understanding the Law of Attraction and the Art of Allowing. Abraham's teachings provide an important understanding of New Thought teachings, and I highly recommend you look into them further.

God Is Inside Us And All Things- This represents a
fundamental shift in man's understanding of God. Prior to this new
age, God was seen as outside of man. Someone to be prayed to.
However, now we know that was not the complete picture. For
God is also inside us. God, or whatever name for God you resonate
with, is in at it's core, the Life Force that permeates the universe.
Otherwise known as Energy. All matter when broken down to its
smallest particles is simply vibrating energy. Thus, God, is in
every cell, in every bit of matter strewn throughout the known and
unknown universe.

There is nowhere that God is not. For many this will be the
hardest part to take in. For this means that God is also in the
tragedies of life. While this is true I've come to understand that
while God Energy is also in my oppressor, it is in there calling him
to reach for a higher vibration, whether or not he is successful. We
must not forget that to God, or to our God Selves we are eternal,
and this is all just one big schoolroom. To my soul, my entire life
span is but a day's lesson.

This God Force is, quite literally, the energy that spins galaxies through space, holds the moon in orbit at night, and yet rotates tiny electrons around tiny atoms. It turns on cellular disease, and it turns it off. At the control seat of this one universal force is THOUGHT. Each thought has a particular vibration, or frequency. Everything inside you, and around you has a particular frequency / vibration. These vibrations can be measured by scientists and the like. They have photographed and measured energy frequencies and vibrational representations in all matter. All objects, living or not living are vibrating. In fact the only difference at the tiniest subatomic level between you and the chair you are sitting in is that you are each vibrating at a different rate of vibration. The truth is that at the smallest subatomic level you are not made up of anything different than the chair!

Biology vs. Biography~ will become the key debate among people in the Great Global Awakening. Some will say that we are our biology. Nothing more, and nothing less. Some will say that we are shaped by our environments to be who we are. These folks will site various case studies that show the effect of the environment on people.

I think that the truth is much more than that. Biology and Biography are not the ends to our understanding of the human psyche, but are merely tools used by Source to express itself. For example, scientists have found that someone who has multiple personalities may have a different internal biology for each of their multiple personalities. At first glance it appears that they are mutually exclusive, however further examination reveals that Source expresses itself sometimes through biology, and sometimes through biography.

Take for example genes. At first glance we see the body made up of genetic blueprints. Everything seems mechanical and repetitive. Yet below the surface are genetic oceans of possibilities, and possible outcomes, that despite billions of people, and trillions of chemical reactions, produce sequences of interactions, of which, no two are alike. Each face is different, each personality is unique. Beneath it all is Source Energy simply, yet magnificently manifesting.

Key to a real understanding of our concept of "reality" is an understanding of bio mechanics. Our eyes were once thought to "see" out into the field in front of us, but science has proven that that is not entirely true. In fact our eyes, and all our sense organs (skin, nose, mouth, and ears) merely decode vibration and light, and then reassemble the perceptions inside our brain, like on a movie screen.

Our sense organs are vibrational interpreters. Our ears interpret vibrational frequency waves into sound for our brains to process. Our eyes translate vibrational frequency waves into visual images. Our nose translates these waves into smells. Our mouth into taste, and our skin into sensations....etc

Like on a movie screen. Our brains then scan the image inside our mind for important information the conscious mind needs. This is why if you are looking for something to happen, you keep seeing it show up in your life. Like noticing that certain numbers keep popping up all day long, or any sign of repetitive patterns.

Scientists have shown that they can implant images on the mind's "screen" and although the object is not there, the subject perceives it as being there physically with everything else. This is also why when Christopher Columbus's ships where coming to shore so many of the Native Americans could not see the ships, until they were pointed out by a shaman, who had advanced skill at seeing. The Native Americans had no previous reference to decode it with visually.

"Seeing is not believing... Instead I will show you that BELIEVING IS SEEING..."

The people ruling society know this, and use media very tactically. It is why your heart pounds when you watch an exciting movie, or your favorite team scores. You feel like you are in the game, because in your mind, you are!

What you decide to believe has happened to you, and around you is what you will see. What you see, you will continue to attract to you, either limitations or limitless possibilities. All based on what you believe. Nothing that is said to us, has any power over us, unless we agree with it. Once we accept the belief as true, it will either build us up, or wear us down. There is only love or fear. I try with each thought to choose love.

The Awakening

Despite so many systems all around the world collapsing, at the same time there appears to be a growing group of people who are waking up to what is really going on. They are waking up to who is manipulating events and who is gaining from them. This is a vast subject and I will be devoting other chapters to covering it in detail. However, for our purpose in this section I will outline some basic information.

Awakened people, developing in greater and greater numbers, understand that they are the change that they have been waiting for. They are learning how to interpret the world around them, and learning to trust their individual interpretations. They no longer trust what they see on TV, because they understand that the media has been bought by the corporate elite to push their ideologies, and cover up their crimes. A small handful of men now own over 96% of the news media around the world.

Awakened people understand that "love thy neighbor" does not mean only the neighbor who looks like you. They understand that countries are man made, and formed to control the masses of people. They see that the politicians do not serve their interests, but instead serve the corporate elite.

In short, they are waking up. Like Neo in The Matrix, they have taken the red pill and are learning just how far down the rabbit hole goes! Dark forces are being brought to the light. Names are being named. Awakened people know who the families were who bought the right to print the money in the United States and around the world. Their sinister schemes to create chaos, like the collapse of the World Trade Center, and the world economy, are being exposed as the inside jobs that they truly are.

Chapter Seven

Understanding The Grid

....On our most basic level, living beings, including human beings, are packets of quantum energy constantly exchanging information with this inexhaustible energy sea.....
- Lynn McTaggert, The Field

Forget Everything You Learned In Science Class

Do you remember your science teachers? Remember the lessons they drilled into your head about atoms, chemical reactions and Newton's Laws....etc. Did you know they were based on theories from the 1600's? Even as they were teaching them to you, researchers were discrediting them and expanding on them. Yet it's not until today that it's all coming together.

Isaac Newton described a world of constants, and predictable outcomes. Those that followed continued the rouse. Charles Darwin, Renee Descartes and many others all came up with theories that described us as separate parts. They would claim that our cells are separate. Our organs are separate. The outer and internal universes are separate. In the Newtonian world we are separate and autonomous from each other.

The church was very powerful and often restricted, or killed scientists. The church would claim control over the world of the unseen, and would allow science to explain the seen world, or physical world. Together, they would hold sway over any new thought.

However by the turn of the last century scientists started finding that we and everything in our world were made up of the same tiny particles. They soon found that those particles where made up of even smaller particles.

Every few years they would find smaller and smaller particles, and then something revolutionary happened. The stuff that made up the smallest particle could not even be called a something. In fact it was more similar to a nothing. This "nothing something" would later be called dark matter.

This dark matter behaved very differently than researchers were use to. In fact there was no consistency to it. The universe was actually a dynamic web of interconnected energy. And that was just the beginning!

For they where finding that things were not separate. Matter was not separate. Time was not separate. Everything was no longer seen as operating separate from any other thing. They further found that not only was everything not separate, but everything was made up of the same things!

Thus we are all interconnected. Some call it a sea, some call it a web, or grid. Although the names differ the idea is the same. Everything is connected, and everything is made up of the same things. The only difference between things is the rate of vibration. So for example, a chair you sit in, is made up of the same subatomic particles as you are. The only difference between you and the chair is your rate of vibration, or frequency. You vibrate within the human frequency, and the chair is vibrating within chair frequencies.

Science reveals to us that we are not the only life forms in the universe. It says that any atom in any planet passing around any star in the universe is as alive as any atom inside me. And that the life force that operates in me also operates through out the universe. Life, on the sub atomic level is everywhere. Like the 1970's song says, we are stardust!

Down By The Quantum Sea

As quantum physics developed it began to split in two different directions. Most scientists explored the devastating power at the sub atomic level. They made ever more powerful bombs and technologically advanced machines. While others dug deeper and unearthed a vast subatomic sea that would later redefine for us what life in the universe is all about.

This second group of scientists found that all the matter in the universe is part of an ocean of microscopic string vibrations in the space between things. These strings made us up, and everything we could see or touch in our universe. All matter contained this same material, only in different variations and vibrating at different speeds. So humans vibrate within certain frequencies, and chairs vibrate at other frequencies, while stars vibrate at still other frequencies. Nothing is "solid", or real, at least to the extent that it cannot be changed.

Learning to harness these vibrations is what becoming a creator is about:

As we think   ----- We feel

As we feel   ----- We vibrate

As we vibrate ----- We attract

A modern scientist, Bruce Lipton, describes Newtonian Physic's information flow with the following formula:

$$A \rightarrow B \rightarrow C$$

While Quantum Physics he describes as :

$$A \leftarrow \rightarrow B \leftarrow \rightarrow C \leftarrow \rightarrow A$$

In Quantum Physics information pathways are holistic, meaning each part affects each part. If "A" was a pharmaceutical drug used to treat "B", we now understand that it will not only effect "B", but will also effect "C". The same effect happens with interactions between people. The thoughts, actions, and energy of person "A" not only effects "B", and visa versa; but also effects person "C", who interacts with "B", whether or not "C" ever physically encounters "A".

We there fore not only can see the power of a positive thought, action, or energy pattern, but we can also see the influence of a negative thought, action or energy pattern. So while quantum physics shows us the power of an individual to affect the whole, it also shows us the responsibility of each part to the whole.

The Grid

The Grid is an interconnected web of energy lines that connect all things to each other. Things once in contact remain in contact across all time and space. In fact these grids shatter even the notion of time and space. The early quantum physicists such as Niels Bohr and others, upon understanding the interconnected treasure chest of knowledge they were opening by delving deeper and deeper into the sub atomic world, eventually came out the other side as philosophers, immersing themselves in the Kabbalah, Chinese Philosophy, and Jungian Psychology.

Once they broke matter down to its tiniest particles they observed that these particles where not made up of any "thing". They found that they were made up of vibrating energy, and what could more be called "nothing", than "something". Within the space between things were microscopic vibrations arranged in a vast quantum field. Lynne McTaggart in a book she called "The

Field" painstakingly reviews what the Grid is and how it was found.

Because of the Grid, what we think and feel is vitally important, not only to ourselves, but even to those around us! Our worlds as we know them are literally constructed from our thoughts. What we believe is exactly what we will see. If we do not believe something, or have no concept of it, than it can be right in front of our faces and we will not see it. There is a story that the Indians did not see Columbus's boat when it first came over the horizon, until one of their shaman spotted it in the bay. The shaman possessed the inner vision necessary to see the ship, without any prior knowledge or experience to aid him in decoding the visual information.

Each moment of our lives our brain decodes millions of bits of information. Some gets sent on to our conscious perceptions, and the rest (the majority) gets stored in our sub conscious mind only to be hinted at in our dreams and intuitions. Our thoughts and feelings also get projected out and add to other's incoming information, and visa versa. Some people will be attracted to these waves, and others will be unaffected or even repelled by them. For most people this happens throughout the day as an unconscious process. For those who are waking up it is becoming more and more of a conscious process.

We walk in and out of each other's fields. Fields collide, and some fields repel. The variations on these interactions are infinite. The interaction gets even more complicated when we take into account the condition of everyone's field. Some fields are very weak, while others are very strong. Some fields have holes in them, while still others have separate energies that have clung to them, known as "parasites".

Shamans have become very good at detecting these "parasites" and extracting them. Today you do not need to go through a long internship with a shaman to work on yourself. Long purification ceremonies are no longer necessary to clean up your own grid. You need only to set the intention, and maintain the belief that it will be so. Soon the universe will find a way to bring it to you. Sometimes in the form you intended, and sometimes in an entirely different form.

It was not always as easy as it is now. In ancient times you did need to perform certain rights, and certain people had to be "called on", and while that still happens today in some rare cases, it is not necessary for the majority of people. The Grid today is so strong, and so pure, that insight and change can happen much more rapidly, and with far greater ease. Today, the power of intention alone is enough to begin to attract your wantings to you.

Ok, so we understand what the Grid is. We know that it connects everything to everything. We know that it transports information day and night, without ever necessarily being seen or felt by most people. We know that there are billions of bits of information being processed by our brains and bodily systems every second, and for the most part they go unnoticed by our conscious mind. For example ultraviolet light is beyond our visual perception, but yet it is affecting us with or without our conscious knowledge.

Everything has its own grid. The earth grid runs through and around the earth. Like the human body there are certain points on the earth grid that can activate energy, heal, or even take energy from one who is in touch with them. Acupuncture has demonstrated these truths in regards to the human body and its use of meridian manipulation. Chinese doctors have long since known that blockages in chi (the body's energy) along certain meridians will lead to weaknesses and ill health. Many say that the earth is sick from all the toxins man has poured into it. The earth grid is working very hard to throw off these toxins but is in continual need of your positive thoughts and energy.

The power of thought, and prayer has been demonstrated to heal at even long distances. Researchers have even seen that the body temperature of a subject can be raised at even long distances by thought and prayer alone. Other experiments have shown that patients who are prayed for even at long distances do better than patients who are not prayed for. The earth needs our thoughts, prayers, and positive energy. It needs vortices and portals opened. Just like cells do better in a health body, we can do better on a healthy planet!

Many unseen forces are becoming recognized by an increasingly technologically advanced society. Electromagnetic Radiation is one unseen force. Some may recall the day when this was once considered "poppy-cock". Today we can measure it with instruments made by men. Each cell in your body gives off electromagnetic radiation. Imagine what can happen when you harness the healing power of billions of these little generators, and focus them in a concerted effort to heal a limb, a breast, or an entire body.

What's The Frequency Kenneth?

The key question left concerning the grid is how does information move along it? The answer looks more and more like it is "frequency". This would explain why two people meet and instantly have chemistry with each other. They are on the same frequency. Once that is established no matter how far you are apart you are able to stay connected. You may find yourself thinking about them, right before they call. It may also explain why a mother feels impending doom at the same time that their child is in trouble.

Cutting edge scientists are finding out more and more that molecules communicate with each other through changes in oscillating frequencies. They are even finding that changes can occur even non locally. By this I mean that scientists are experimenting with tape recording healing sound frequencies from certain molecules, and sending them by mail around the world to scientists in other countries and finding measurable changes in diseased animals when the sound is played to the new molecules.

This is opening up whole new fields of study and medicine. Light is being studied, to understand the how light frequencies can heal. Water is being studied to understand how frequency effects water molecules, and how they can benefit people. Healing sounds are being researched, and the benefits recorded and sent around the globe.

Traditional allopathic medicine continues to try and thumb their nose, but one by one, each of the therapies that were once attributed to charlatans are slowly gaining acceptance, first by the patients, and then eventually by the doctors themselves. I think it is clear that the future of medicine and imaging technologies comes down to one word, "frequency"!

Water molecules seem to be particularly good at tape recording, imprinting, and carrying information. It does not come as any surprise that our bodies are mostly water, or the success of homeopathy whose solutions contain mostly water. The human brain is also much better at memory than we were ever aware.

Do you realize that your brain remembers everything? Every event that ever happened to you gets stored in an engram, or particular cell in the brain. When experimenters in the 1920's stimulated spots on subjects brains specific events were recalled in vivid detail. These experiments have been replicated again and again. The result is the same, we all have excellent memories, it's just that some people have better recall ability than others. Today we also know that each memory, is not only stored in a separate engram, but is connected by dendritic branches to all other parts of the brain.

Frequencies, or tiny charges, lead to waves of electrical cascades throughout the brain, that lead to recall, and all thought. What mechanism processes these masses of excitations? That became the key concern for researchers? Like Dorothy trying to find who, and where the Wizard was?

The answer comes in understanding that the brain receives information through holographic transformation of wave interference patterns. Memory, and the mechanisms for it is distributed all over the brain, and as Candice Pert would later show, all over the body, for cells have their own individual memory, and agendas.

Finally there are appearing proven alternatives to taking drugs to get better. Alternative technologies are now forming that will allow us to get rid of unwanted pathogens through the use of frequency modulation. We no longer have to use harmful pesticides, but will one day be able to kill parasites with electromagnetic signals. Lynn McTaggert concludes her study of the grid by saying the following in perhaps the most concise way I've ever read:

" A substructure underpins the universe that is essentially a recording medium for everything, providing a means for everything to communicate with everything else. People are indivisible from their environment. Living consciousness is not an isolated entity. It increases order in the rest of the world. The consciousness of human beings has incredible powers to heal ourselves, to heal the world – in a sense, to make it as we wish it to be".

Lies My Father Told Me

I don't recall what my thesis was for my Master's degree, but my unofficial thesis was a collection of essays I put together for my final class with Professor McAndrews. I called it "Lies My

Father Told Me". It was not written about an actual father I had, but in general "father" represented society, and the white, male power structure that runs it.

Most of these people where not, "bad" people. They were simply repeating "tapes" that they heard their "fathers" repeat to them. We are all collectively part of the problem. The only way to end this is by thinking new thoughts. Anything we believe, could be an illusion, and may not be real, or factual. We must have the courage to be flexible with any of our beliefs.

On an individual level we must each reclaim our minds for ourselves. Only by doing this can we become our potential selves. This is the only way to find peace in the world, or ourselves. Peace in the world through peace in ourselves. We cannot look to presidents, or so called leaders, because they do not have peace inside them any more than you do, and so they cannot give it to anyone else. We cannot look to our priests, or holy books as transcribed through man, for our own truth. Only our direct experience will light our paths. People can help us, but the final litmus test must be our own.

The first belief we need to re examine is our belief about "enemy". If we are all from the same source both physically through genetics, and spiritually, through Source energy, and if the differences in our genetics and biology are virtually unrecognizable, then who is the enemy? We are all from the same family. There is only one race, the human race. The idea of different races, is a lie.

Could you kill a family member? Would you let your brother starve? Once you truly understand that we are all one being and that you do not end at the tips of your fingers and toes, you can end your war with others outside yourself. When you can come to accept that the universe is a fully conscious, alive, being. When you accept that you are a contributing consciousness within the greater consciousness. That you are here with unique gifts, abilities, and destinies. When you can feel Source moving through you, and everything there is. Then you will be ready to end the race.

End your "race – ing"! You do not have to worry about losing anything to anyone else that's really important. For your true essence cannot be given away to anyone, and no one can take it from you. The worst fate that you, or anyone can hold over you is death, and death is a lie! There is no such thing. One thing all scientists agree on is that at our core we are energy. The second thing all scientists agree on is that energy never dies. You are Source, and you will return to it again one day.

They Shoot Horses Don't They

When a horse is lame or hurt, it is thought of as humane to shoot the horse. For the horse will never walk or "trot" again. There is no hope for his recovery. This is also true of the mess of lies and falsehoods we have embedded in our psyche. This is often done as a defense mechanism. So many things come up in life that we are just not ready to face. So we found alternative routes that were easier on us. Usually they are routes that avoided the problem all together.

Do not blame yourself for this. It was in the past and is already done. So many people when they reach this point feel so much guilt; myself included. The important thing is that you try to breakthrough your defenses. There is victory in the trying.

Source will respond to your trying. This is "grace". You will feel stronger and more in control of your life. An inner peace will be noticed more and more.

Modern psychology has failed the average person. If you are not psychotic, or neurotic there is not much help for you from psychologists. This is where Liberation Psychology is able to step in. By becoming creators in our life we begin to grow these stuck parts of ourselves. Leaving our defenses behind, we see ourselves in a new light. Stretching out through experiences, guided by Source on an internal level, and learning to find, and trust our own inner guidance.

On an external level becoming one with others and all of creation lifts us into fully experiencing the beauty of our being. Source will be found both inside us and outside of us. If you have tasted Source you know that it was there all along. Behind the stillness inside of love. We passed it to others a thousand times, and we sat with it in our most profound moments.

Modern psychology had no name for it before now. If you are considered mentally stable then life is suppose to be fine, and they need do nothing to help you. We bought the delusion that there are a few listable stages of mental illness or mental health.

In reality there are over 7 billion stages of mental health/illness. One for every man, woman, and child. For we all had uniquely different experiences in our life. Some are more developed in some areas, and weaker in other areas. We don't even stay in a particular stage. What stage we are at can fluctuate throughout the day. We might be in a relatively strong and confident space, when we hear a comment about us, and instantly we regress back, sometimes several stages back. This goes on all the time, and sometimes we are expanding, and other times we are regressing.

Love does not care which "stage" we are at. It is always waiting for us. It's beside you right now. You need only ask for it. You do not have to be holy, or celibate, or climb up a high mountain. You do not have to go through the seven water tortures, to make yourself pure. Love is at your call, and always was. I wasted years believing the fallacy that God would be revealed to me if I only asked for him the right way, or did what someone else told me I needed to do to make myself worthy.

The bullet to shoot that "horse" with is "we are born ready". Love is where we came from, and where we will return when we die. Divinity is your birthright. At least it was until you gave it away to someone else. Someone who told you how to pray, and what was right and wrong.

Put down this book, for a moment and take back your birthright. Claim your role as creator in your own life. For your first act as creator reclaim your divinity. Bestow love permanently in your life.

The Family of Man

Look around you. Can you feel it? Can you feel the change coming? Can you at least feel it in you? Slowly, one person at a time, people are waking up to the understanding. Everything around us is all one, and we are all one. One scientific discovery after another is gently guiding even the most sluggish of us from our slumber. Gently guiding us from the illusion of our separateness.

Dr. Joseph Graves Jr. wrote a recent book called "The Race Myth". In it he discussed the latest findings that early man first developed in Africa around 3.5 million years ago. During this time there were several groups or "species" existing together in Africa. The species that is today the modern man eventually won out, and around 250,000 years ago there remained just one.....Us!

This species is called Homo Sapiens, and roughly 60,000 years ago began leaving the rift valley in Africa, and spreading all around the world. What this means is that every human being traces their ancestry back to Africa. Scientists have found that 99.9% of the genes inside of people are the same as the ones inside their neighbor. Out of 22,000 types of human genes there are only 6 that are responsible for skin color. That is all that makes us different.

We've been feeding beliefs of separateness far too long. The facts are finally in, and the time has come for us to grasp our oneness, and a true understanding of our place in All That Is. The universe is expanding. Love is growing. Little by little each and every one of us is coming home.

Sometimes there will be resistance. Sometimes those who are still tied to a pain body will try and damper your light. Sometimes there will be wars and rumors of war. However the path of mankind is upward. Just like the path of All That Is, is also upward. Like the great Martin Luther King Jr. said: "I've been to the mountaintop…and I've seen the promised land. I may not get there with you, but we as a people will get to the promised land". The individual personalities that we each are now, may not reach enlightenment, or be able to stay connected to Source every moment of the day. However you can take solace that "we" will all get there eventually one day.

Creation Stories

Our ancestors in the Rift Valley, and every civilization that sprang from them had their own creation story. Many with similar themes. For example like the Christian, and Jewish religions the Dogon tribe in Africa tell an ancient story of God deciding to create man directly. They however, also speak of the importance of the Pleiades, the "long tailed star, in the belt of Orion. As I heard these stories I experienced an inner knowing. I am not able to

117

verbalize the importance of these stories, nor give reason for their close similarity.

It is not talked about in the west much, but our African ancestors understood and passed down technologically advanced knowledge about the world around them. For example the Dogon understood what today we call String Theory. String Theory basically says that if you broke down the smallest particles you will find that they are made up of energy, in the form of a small string like structure that vibrates. How each of these tiny strings vibrates determines what the composition of the piece of matter will be. So if the string vibrate one way, it will be a chair, and if the strings vibrate another way it will be a person. If we take this even further we will understand that the strings in a cancer cell vibrate a certain way, and the strings in non cancerous cells would vibrate slightly differently.

The Dogon pass their knowledge down in the form of stories that are symbolic in nature, yet exact in their science. They tell of objects that are made up of smaller objects, that are made up of smaller objects, even down to the sub atomic level. And that these objects are made up of tiny coils. Perhaps these "coils" represent

118

the vibrating strings? One day we will be able to isolate strings in the lab and know for sure who is more accurate.

We are just now coming to understand the multifaceted powers of water. How it too is vibrating, and emitting frequencies. We now know that we can influence its crystalline structure simply with the power of our thoughts, and that the water seems to actually act as a recorder of the frequency of our thought.

"Vibes"

The old hippy adage "He's sending me good vibes", or "He's sending me bad vibes", is really not that far from the truth. Today we have instruments that can pick up and display vibration for us. They do this by transforming vibration into frequency. These noninvasive scanning technologies can scan us and our energy fields and analyze our frequency changes.

Our vibrational energy waves not only effect internal interactions on the subatomic level, but also effect interpersonal relationships on the external level. By "picking up" another person's "vibes" we are reacting to our perception of the frequency they are emitting. Animals who are not encumbered by an ego rely extensively on being able to quickly interpret the vibration of oncoming beings.

The medical community found that there could be uses of "constructive interference" mechanics to treat such things as kidney stones by using harmonic frequency. Doctors can non invasively focus harmonic resonance waves and target them to the kidney stones. The resulting congruence keeps increasing the rate of vibration until the stone explodes.

Our bodies are wired, specially our brains, as beings of electricity and light. That is why electric shock could seem to be so successful. Our bodies are continually conducting electricity, vibrating, and sending out energy waves. The body is not separate from the mind. The mind is not separate either. Get rid of the old idea that the conscious and subconscious minds are separate. Yes, they have their own individual roles, but like spokes on a wheel, they work together to keep you going.

Higher organisms developed more and more intricate brains. Scientists have found that most of our higher order thinking comes from our Prefrontal Cortex. This allows for the development of highly complex behavioral patterns. These aide in our ability to quickly learn and adapt, sometimes even without prior experience.

It's A Small World After All

Who would have thunk it? Who would have thought that the world of the large is so strikingly similar to the world of the small? By large I mean solar systems and galaxies. By small I mean sub atomic particles and vibrating strings. Amazingly, scientific discoveries are showing us that the world of the small is getting smaller, and the world of the big is getting bigger and bigger, when it comes to our understanding of each.

Much like our Dogon friends in Africa, we are finding out that just when we think we have found our place in the galaxy we find that our galaxy is within a cluster of galaxies. If that's not daunting enough we find that each cluster of galaxies is within a super cluster....and it goes on and on.

Likewise the world of the small gets smaller and smaller with each new discovery. For example each of the 7 billion people on this planet has tens of trillions of cells in their body. Each of those cells has hundreds of thousands of neuro chemicals making an infinite number of reactions every second. Each of which is made up of sub atomic particles spinning in particular patterns, all of which is controlled by seas of tiny strings that make up these smallest particles.

One would be overwhelmed trying to comprehend the awesome power of the world of large forces, and the microscopic intricacies of the world of the small. For me this is where my faith in God comes in. For I know that if I cannot yet comprehend "how" the dance of the universe works, it does not mean that I cannot take part in it.

Chapter Eight

Source Energy

528 hz - The God Frequency –
5 senses (see, hear, touch, taste, and smell) –
2 energies (light and sound) –
8 letters "I love you" resonate heart sounds healing
cellular structures through VIBRATION....

~ Kazi Kearse

Sensing Source Energy

Einstein was describing " Source" energy. It is very difficult to explain it to someone, and much, much easier to have them experience it for themselves. Before we begin this work, we must first find a personal relationship with Source.

Source is the energy in the universe that creates worlds. Each of us will have different words to describe it. God, Love, Joy…etc. I call it "Joy Love" for short. You may have your own words for it. Do not try and come up with them, however, before you have a direct experience with Source. Once you do have that direct experience with Source you will have your own words, even if your words are "it's beyond words"!

You can experience Source, anytime, at will. You may use a partner to assist you in reaching it, or you can do it on your own. The important thing is that you quite the mind and keep going deeper, and deeper beyond each thought or sensation you feel or imagine.

The following is based on The Journey Process as taught by Brandon Bays. She is a wonderful healer and teacher who has expanded working with Source Energy to use it to do self therapy. I highly recommend that you look into her work after this brief "taste of Source".

STEP ONE:

Close your eyes and get comfortable either sitting or laying down. When you get a feeling or sensation bring all your attention to it. Feel where in the body the feeling or sense calls home. Allow it to grow stronger. Ask yourself, what is beneath this feeling or sensation?

What's at the core of it? Then relax, and open into it. Keep opening to it, until you arrive at what is beneath the feeling or sensation...and then do the same for this new feeling or sensation.

Keep doing this until you arrive at the core. It is not unusual to find that certain people show up in our visions here. If a person shows up simply note this and continue going deeper.

STEP TWO:

Eventually, you will arrive at Source. You will know you are there by a feeling of overwhelming vastness, love, joy, freedom. It has many names but the feeling is distinct and undeniable. You will know you are there when you are there!

When I first tasted Source I was so filled with Joy / Love that I wanted to run out of the workshop room. I experienced Source visually as a fiery orb, perhaps the size of a million galaxies, shining and blazing in the middle of the universe. It was intelligent and had thoughts emanating from it.

STEP THREE:

Ask the Source you found to speak to you in words. Be sure to write them down. You may return here anytime you want.

Welcome home....

Law Of Creation

= Law of Attraction

= "That which is likened onto itself is drawn"

(Abraham) from Ask and It Is Given

Working With Source Energy

Step 1: Go To Your Power Place

A Power Place is a special place that you find where you feel particularly comfortable, and at peace. A place that feels safe yet tremendously empowering. It is a place you find (or finds you) that resonates with your vibration.

You will need to find such a place in your physical world. However, until you do, it is perfectly fine to create a similar place in your mind. It is vital that it become absolutely real to you, and all your senses. So pay particular attention to remembering the feel of the place, the smells, the scenery. Pay attention to every detail. The more powerfully you are able to recall it, the more effective the power of your intention will be.

Step 2: State Your Intention

The first step in creating change in your life and attracting to you the things you desire is to simply state them. You must state them out loud, to the universe. This is how you will let Source know what it is you want from it. It can take the form of speaking your intention out loud, writing it down, painting a picture...etc. Whatever you feel called to do. The object is to express the intention to Source.

You will find that like a magnet, you are attracting to you what it is you spend the predominance of your thoughts on. The more intense you can make your thoughts, the brighter their energy is seen, and the stronger their vibration is felt, and heard, on the other side.

There is a multitude of help available to us from the universe. We are supported by so many people and things that we take for granted, such as our neighbors and community members. From the paper boy, to the guy up on the electric pole. From our lungs that breathe us, to the sun that holds us in its mighty orbit. All is supporting you always.

Whether you send the thoughts to God, your Ancestors, Buddha, Allah, Christ, or the Devil, you will receive back that which you ask for. All is Source, and all taps into Source. Source does not judge the "correctness" of your thought. The lessons we learn are our journeys. We will deliver the lessons, and the journeys back to Source one day!

All too often, misguided, or poorly formed thoughts yield equally negative outcomes for us. We wallow in these thoughts, and thus project them out even more intensely. It is easy to see how a snowball effect can get started. We call it "a string of bad luck" or "a period of depression", but the causes are the same.

The good news is that we can derail any snowball, anytime that we stop feeding it thoughts. When we simply begin to nurture new thoughts, we set in motion completely new outcomes.

Set aside some time now to try it. What is it that you would like to manifest more in your life? Is it something you would like to do? What do you wish to attract more of? Is there an area in your life were you would like to see more abundance?

I will list some of mine, only to act as an example of what you can ask for. These have worked for me, but it is important that you choose your own, and state them in your own words. After you have done that it will be important that you break the intention down into steps, or "Sub Intentions":

Example- Intention: Increase Joy/ Love in my family...

Sub Intentions:

1. Spend more time together.

2. Have more fun together.

3. We will listen more to each other.

Example- Intention: I want to make more money.

Sub Intentions:

1. I will attract unlimited financial abundance.

2. I am a money magnet!

3. I have an unlimited bank account.

Example- Intention: I want to understand my purpose in life.

Sub Intentions:

1. I want to make more of a difference.

2. I want greater self knowledge.

3. I seek a closer relationship with higher beings.

Example- Intention: I want to find more love in my life.

Sub Intentions:

1. I will attract only those who are in harmony.

2. I am ready to love without limits or boundaries, and I do not contain preconceived expectations of what that love will look like.

3. I am allowing love into my life.

How do you find this little exercise? Is it hard? It should be, and if it wasn't than it will be! For the task of re creating your life is not a simple one. It will get easier as you have more and more experiences with Source, but I will not try to kid you that it's all fun and games. Friends may turn on you, and loved ones may be very resentful of the changes you make.

It will be necessary for you to dig up and uncover your deepest shadows. And I know all too well, that they do not like to be uncovered. See, they were driven down there by fear, and they have become all mangled and contorted, yet oddly enough, comfortable.

Some might question why we even bother to unearth them, but we cannot fully dance without them. Even the largest room is never completely dark again once just a single match is lit!

Some parts of ourselves have become cut off or disassociated with our main personality. Under extreme trauma a part may split off entirely. But do not worry, because love is the most powerful energy in the universe and we will reclaim these lost parts, one by one, on our way home. I used a shamanism process called Soul Retrieval to gather these lost essences of myself.

We do Soul Retrievals many times, without even knowing it. One time when I was barely 20 years old my girlfriend went through a traumatic experience and became catatonic. Meaning her brain "froze" and she lost all expression and communication with the outside world. It's like the person is just a shell. However I held her and prayed to the holiest thing I knew at the time, Jesus, to help us. I repeated the words "The power of Christ commands you to return", over and over again. It had worked once for me in a dream during another crisis, and lo and behold it actually worked for me in "real" life too! As I repeated the words over and over she came out of her catatonia in moments.

Buddha knew this to be true thousands of years ago. He said:

" We are what we think.

With our thoughts we make the world".

Today quantum physics has proven this to be absolutely true. Our world, our reality, is a sea of potentials. We truly can create with it what we want. Thus, this is a guidebook for creators. People who are ready to step up to mold their own destiny!

Step3: Allow Source To Respond

Allowance is perhaps the most difficult step, because so much of our baggage gets involved in it. Allowance is an attitude. We achieve it when we stop offering resistance to the current our life wishes to go in.

"It is very difficult to explain this feeling to anyone who is entirely without it, especially as there is no anthropomorphic conception of God corresponding to it. The individual feels the nothingness of human desires and aims, and the sublimity and marvelous order which reveal themselves both in nature and the world of thought. He looks upon individual existence as a sort of prison and wants to experience the universe as a single significant whole"

- Albert Einstein (The World As I See It)

Creation Formula

$$Creation = A + B + C$$
$$(Ask) \quad (Believe) \quad (Co\text{-}Sign)$$

A: *Ask the universe for what you want:* This is the first step. The louder, and more often the better. You should speak the words, write the words down in a journal, basically tell everyone you possibly can, and in everyway you can.

B: *Believe that the universe will deliver to you exactly what you are wanting:*
You must believe this with all your heart. In your mind you must act as if you already have what you are wanting. Based on the Law Of Attraction the universe will bring you all things of like vibration.

C: *Co-Sign on to what you are being delivered:*
You must go get what you were asking for, and be ready to receive it. Your life needs to be set up to receive what you are asking for. You must then be willing to go to the door and receive the package that is waiting for you. So many people make the mistake of asking for something, but forgetting to open the door to let it in. Your life must become an environment that can support the vibration of what you are asking for. So you must be ready to make the necessary pre changes to your life to be ready for the major changes you are wanting. This is all part of Co-Signing.

Chapter Nine

The New Energy Technologies

"The mind is like an iceberg, it floats with one-seventh its bulk above water"
- Sigmund Freud

Energy Psychology

It was not long after I came to fully understand the grid, and what source is, that I began to ask myself the fundamental question. To me, the fundamental question became what happens when we take conscious control over our thoughts? Can we develop a psychology or system to physically manifest our mental thoughts? Is there a way to consciously cultivate subconscious resources towards fulfilling our goals and desires?

The answer to all the above questions is YES! To my surprise I didn't even have to reinvent the wheel. Much of the work had already been begun by other researchers. Men like Bruce Lipton, and women like Candice Pert, helped point me in the right direction. They showed that beliefs not only control behavior, but help shape our genes.

Where does the mind - body relationship end? How far down the rabbit hole can we go with this? The foundation for energy psychology goes back some 4,500 years. We know that even the Buddha taught that we are what we think, and he clearly understood the relationship of our thoughts over our physical world.

Modern day researchers and practitioners are developing the use of scientific equipment and principles to study and harness subtle energy fields in and around all living things. In this chapter we will deal mainly with the human body, but it's important that you understand that all living things have subtle energy fields. Early researchers found out that when they took Kirlian Photography pictures of plants they would notice that the way they spoke to or interacted with the plants effected the images on the film.

Some have even begun to find that water molecules take different shapes based upon the thoughts that are sent to them. This has far reaching effects on our understanding of human potential since our bodies are around 70% water. The findings from these investigations shout out a new paradigm. They prove to us all that thoughts are not just mental events, but also are physical events. Thoughts have energy, both electrically and chemically. These energies can be studied, and ultimately one can learn to manipulate them.

Modern science is beginning to use these new technologies more and more in our everyday world. Chiropractic and Acupuncture treatments are now reimbursable by many health insurance companies. These treatments use techniques based upon the manipulation of blockages in nerve impulses and chi within the human biofield.

Brain Imaging technology can now display for us exactly how changes in thoughts directly correspond with electrical and chemical changes in the brain. For example, if you think about emotion A, the area in the brain corresponding to A lights up on the screen. Then if you suddenly change your thought to emotion B, area B in the brain will light up, as area A dims.

Any electrical current creates an electromagnetic field. Every cell in our body contains many electrical charges with usually one dominant overall charge, either positive or negative, based on the sum and type of charges. Each cell becomes like a little battery, and as David Feinstein states in his many books on Energy Psychology, we each have about 75 trillion of these little batteries going on and off all day long.

At the molecular level we are not one single individual but instead we are actually a vast community of sub atomic energy with hundreds of thousands of members growing, transforming, and even dying, every second. Our minds cannot even grasp the number of members multiplied 7 billion times, that we would have, for every man, woman, and child. Yet we walk through this ocean of potential everyday. Sending out thoughts, and receiving energy constantly, all day long.

To help us navigate these vast interactions, Energy Psychology can play an important role. We can begin by examining the flow of subtle energy. This energy flows throughout the universe. At the macro level, it hurls galaxies through space and at the micro level it moves energy throughout your body. If you have ever been lucky enough to have felt this subtle energy flow through you in our earlier exercise with Source, you do not need me to describe it further, but for people who have not, I can describe it simply as a gentle current that flows throughout everything. By the end of this book you will have had the chance to experience it again, but do not put too much pressure on yourself to feel it physically yet. Give your mind a chance to grasp the concept and play with it a while. I did not feel it for a long time and then suddenly I felt it one day during a meditation, when I was ready to. There are no mistakes in this universe. Things have a way of happening at the exact right time.

When energy is flowing through the mind we feel good. When there are blockages either due to fear, or other causes, the brain enters fight or flight mode. Keep in mind your Psych 101 lessons on Pavlov's Dog, and how memories about thoughts can produce physical realities, such as salivating, long after the object is gone.

In Energy Psychology we bring the psychological problem to mind and stimulate the energy meridian points on the body that counteract the brain's threat response. By doing this the nervous system gets retrained to handle the psychologically stressful condition.

Any person getting up from a chiropractors table will tell you the relief they feel when their body is in alignment. The use of energy meridians in Chinese medicine has been used by Chinese doctors for centuries, and even in the modern hospitals of today. There are 14 major meridians, and each has a location on the body that when tapped, unblock, and move energy.

Gary Craig developed a system he calls the Emotional Freedom Technique (EFT) which uses 8 meridian points and the repeating of a specific reminder phrase. First it is necessary to recall the feeling of the problem you want to work on. The more vivid you make the recall the better. You then begin tapping the points and repeating your reminder phrase so as to hold the energy of the emotion present. This activates the psychological, emotional, and neuro chemical components of the problem. A bridging sequence is also used that involves eye movements coincided with specific hand tapping. This is followed by more rounds of tapping along with a reminder phase. The session ends when the person's fear reaction is down to 0.

I know that this sounds bizarre, even the developers admit to that, but the fact is it works, and people all over the world are receiving help from it. It is perhaps the future of psychology in the 21st century. It's counterpart, Energy Medicine, is equally effective and equally promising.

Body – Mind Energy

There is no longer any doubt that our bodies hold innate knowledge and wisdom that we are only beginning to tap into. Applied Kinesiology developed by Dr. George Goodheart shows us that certain Indicator Muscles can tell us whether the item we are holding is good or bad for us. His pioneering work was followed by Dr. John Diamond, who found that you could get the same results with emotional and intellectual stimuli. He called this Behavioral Kinesiology.

Proper training is needed to master these skills however the basic steps require two people to work together. The first person, we'll call the subject, stands up and holds their left arm straight out. The second person, we'll call the researcher, places their left hand on the subject's right shoulder, and their right hand on the subject's extended left arm just above the wrist. The researcher then tells the subject to resist them trying to push the subject's arm down.

If their arm stays up the muscle is testing strong in regard to the object being held, or thought being spoken. If the muscle is weak the researcher will be able to push the subject's arm down with some ease. As David Hawkins MD. explains in his ground breaking book, Power vs Force, this technique has stood the test of time and has shown to be predictable, and repeatable with people of many different ages and backgrounds.

There are also various ways of muscle testing yourself. It is ok to use these self test techniques if a partner is not available, or if you want to ask yourself a quick question regarding your subconscious beliefs. You can also use it if you want to quickly check if something is good for you.

What you do is touch the tips of your thumb and pointer fingers together, on each hand. Form two circles, and then bring them together forming interlocking circles. You then choose one hand to pull, and one hand to resist. It's best to use your least dominant had to resist, and your dominant hand to pull. Ask a question, and then slowly pull the fingers on your dominant hand away from your fingers on your less dominant hand. See if the circle breaks. A yes answer will test strong, and your fingers on your less dominate hand will give way. A no answer will be when the fingers on your dominant hand cannot get released.

The Standing Pendulum process is a third way to muscle test. This process combines the ability to hold the item you want to test, and the quickness and convenience of being able to do this work without having to have a partner. To do it, you stand up straight. If you are holding an item that you would like to test, place it against you, in your solar plexus region between your upper stomach, and lower chest area. Think of a question, and verbalize it out loud.

You will then begin to feel your body want to tilt in a certain direction. You will feel a pull forward or backwards. A pull forward is a positive response to your question. Your body / higher self / God force, is telling you that it feels favorable about the item in question. A pull backwards is a weak, or negative response from your body / higher self/ God force, and means that the item in question is not good for you.

You can do this with questions you have, or to access your innate knowing about a person, place or thing. For example, if you are unsure of your feelings towards someone, you can hold a picture of them, write their name down on a piece of paper, or simply say their name out loud. Your body will either move forward, if they are good for you, or your body will tilt backwards if they are not good for you.

Robert Williams takes muscle testing a bit further by using it as a tool to aid personal development. His Psych-K method uses the latest brain research to reprogram your subconscious mind with your conscious desires. This type of cognitive reprogramming is not only promising for individuals looking to develop new thoughts and behaviors, but it may be capable of lifting all of humanity one day. By groups of people focusing their thoughts on love, the potential exists for developing the beginning of a unified consciousness.

The concept of a unified consciousness has been much sought after by people all around the world, and throughout time. You can also unify your own consciousness. It has gone by many names: meditation, prayer, Zen, etc…All of these traditions seek to quite the mind and bring the conscious and subconscious together.

Begin first by finding out your subconscious beliefs. These beliefs can lead to resistance to your desires. How often do you make the intent to bring more of something into your life, only to be thwarted by a subconscious belief that you are not good enough for it? These would also be called your self sabotaging beliefs. No matter how strong your power of intention is you will not be able to attract anything of value to you unless you dig up these subconscious beliefs.

Be easy with yourself as you uncover these subconscious beliefs. You can begin by muscle testing yourself, and your reaction to certain core belief statements. It's important to always address the statement in the positive, and to speak out loud. Pay attention to which beliefs test strong, and which test weak.

Sample Questions:

1. "I believe in God".

2. "I believe God loves me".

3. "I love myself unconditionally".

4. " I am ready for more love in my life".

5. " I deserve to have all the money I need".

6. " I feel safe, secure, and confident in the world".

Key to learning to consciously control the forces of the universe is understanding the role of meaning. When we do not have meaning we lose the will to live. When our lives are meaningful we are in our power. When someone is in their power they have a strong life force. Other people easily pick up on it, even on a subconscious level.. These people can live to a ripe old age, and remain fruitful and contributing to the world around them..

Learn to stalk power. Stalking Power is an indigenous technique that shaman have trained each other to do for centuries. It is done by quieting the mind and manipulating your own frequency to come into alignment with the power, or frequency of the object or area. Some power has been left behind. Some power is actively searching for stalkers. Some are benevolent, some are not so. However no energy can come within your field if you do not resonate with it on some level.

You do this by developing your impeccability. Particularly the impeccability of your word. Words are strong vibrators, and useful tools. It is important to stay focused on your goals. Focus is vital, and will be called on during every step of your stalking power. The ability to quite your mind needs to be developed. Much like a weight lifter develops their physique. Only with a quite mind does the prey hear the hunter approaching. If the prey is in fear and fleeting, it will not hear the coming attack, and can make no adjustment.

The question is not to become a master at the art of stalking. The task is to become a master, and the stalking ability will follow. Learn to let Source flow through you. You need to be able to tap into it at will, store it, and send it when needed. Be able to develop strong visualization ability. The stronger the visualization the stronger the frequency and vibration will be. Above all, when you are learning to stalk power know that you will have to practice it. Frequent practice leads to knowledge, knowledge leads to clarity, and clarity leads to power.

Chapter Ten

The Mechanics Of Feelings

Every feeling, every thought, every emotion we experience sends a message to each cell in the body...
- Karol Truman

Emotional Jihad

Love is funny. It doesn't necessarily stick in one place forever. No matter how hard we try to make the damn thing stick, the edges keep coming up after awhile! Anxiety has a way of sneaking in. It requires an emotional jihad to out wit, out last, and out perform your own self doubt.

I must be ready to confront feelings and ideas within myself that are ugly, buried, and otherwise dark. This is your Shadow. I will discuss the shadow in much more detail coming up in other parts of the book. But for now just know that love can be welcomed by the shadow (eventually), and can transform even the shadow. In return, your shadow will allow you to receive the loving, and tender aspects of yourself.

A Jihad is a holy war. An Emotional Jihad is a prolonged love action. Whereby love gets infused in your bloodstream, and the darkness inside you melts away. To do this you will need the following weapons:

-Courage

- A Journal

- Processing with one or more persons.

Courage is the rock that you will build your new world on. It's a courage that knows that there is nothing to fear. It's a faith in love. For what is the worst that they can do to you? When we are able to redefine death, we can see it as part of a natural process of change, and transition. Death itself is not so scary. If there is no life after death, then you will not be in any pain. And if there is life after death then you can enjoy yourself in heaven. It's a win - win situation!

You must remember that you are an eternal being! This means that the consciousness that is YOU will not end when this life does. For example, each night you close your eyes and your conscious mind shuts off. Yet the YOU that is you, continues. You may not remember the dream when you wake, but you know that you were dreaming. You know that YOU where somewhere else. You know that you continued on without your present body. You do it each night, and you will do it in death. Do not fear, you will drift into your next life as surely as you slip between dreams.

Your journal can be an important tool in remembering love. Love heals, but a good journal is the injector. In our past we have had many traumas, both big and small. During each of these traumas a part of us gets taken by the Shadow and placed somewhere in our psyche that is safe. It is usually somewhere that is far away from our conscious mind, that was experiencing the trauma.

Freedom

As Ray Dodd says in his book Belief Works, "Be the prize, that you are seeking after". There is no need to look for anything outside ourselves. You are free to be the love you are looking for in another, the peace you hope for in your family, or the parent you never had.

Shamans are masters of both the waking world and the non waking world, otherwise known as non ordinary reality. Both worlds are seen as dream states. You are dreaming right now, even as you are reading my words. Like your non waking dreams you fill your waking mind with all your perceptions. You and everyone in your dream has defined roles and expectations.

When a shaman achieves mastery they escape their dream and walk in and out of both worlds with freedom. They are able to exercise personal choice in each world. They remain aware in either world. They are able to manipulate their reality in each world according to their desires. They are free!

This same freedom awaits you. It will not cost you a cent, nor require great degrees. Your life will become art, and you will be the artist. In this new found freedom there is nothing that you cannot be, do , or have.

Does this freedom scare you? Do not be afraid, for there are no wrong turns. There are only lessons, and adjustments to lessons. Always keep in mind that you, and only you, are responsible for your choices, and no one else's. Remember the role of the Law Of Attraction, and the fact that reality in your world will follow your beliefs, intentions, and desires (your thoughts).

You Are Living Your Thoughts

- "I will never be rich"

- "I do not deserve love"

- "I am stuck here forever"

- "I am fat"

These are just some of the many thoughts that we hold about ourselves. They will remain true for us as long as we choose to believe them. To change our beliefs we must practice new ones. We must practice them until we believe these new beliefs. For that is exactly how your old beliefs got put there.

Our beliefs are vital because it is the beliefs that radiate the vibrations. The vibrations will attract people and events to us. We begin this by picturing what we want. However you need to do this you must do it, and as often as possible. So for example, if you want to attract riches, put up pictures of people with riches. If you want to attract love, put up pictures of the type of mate, or relationship you want. If you feel you are fat put up healthy looking pictures. Bring these images into your vibration, and your vibration into these images.

Who are the people, and circumstances that are in your life right now? They reflect your current beliefs. I know some of you will have a hard time accepting this, but remember that I am speaking only about "beliefs", not wants, or wishes. You may want to be rich, but believe you cannot be. You may wish to find love, yet believe that you never will.

The key is to start a new dream. There is a term I talk about in this book called lucid dreaming. It is what happens when someone wakes up inside their dream at night. Ray Dodd describes Lucid Living as when we are awake during our daytime dream, or awake life. Like lucid dreamers, we become awake to the fact that we are dreaming, and are able to make choices in our dream. The only difference is that we are doing it in our waking life.

10 Feeling States

1. Love / Joy

2. Happiness

3. Optimism

4. Contentment

5. Frustration

6. Blame

7. Anger

8.. Revenge

9. Hatred/ Rage

10. Fear/ Despair/ Powerlessness

I see the ten feeling states as a hierarchical staircase. Love /
Joy is the highest feeling state, and Fear / Despair/ Powerlessness
are the lowest. I will give you a short description of each state:

10 Feeling States

1. Love / Joy :	Feeling loved and connected to everything. Extreme Pleasure.
2. Happiness:	Excitement at being alive.
3. Optimism:	Hopefulness about future.
4. Contentment:	Satisfaction.
5. Frustration	Discontentment with the way things are.
6. Blame:	Feeling that someone or something is the cause of the problem.
7. Anger:	Being upset at a particular person, or situation.
8. Revenge	Feeling upset with someone and wanting to get them back.
9. Hatred / Rage	Extreme dislike. To the point of wanting to do violence.
10. Fear / Despair /Powerlessness	Severe feelings of lack of safety or worth.

The key is moving up the list, choosing increasingly more productive thoughts. People who practice this can learn to recognize negative thoughts, or thoughts that do not serve them. They then can search, and find new thoughts that serve them better. The more you practice it, the better you get at it. Until one day, it becomes effortless, and part of who you now are!

Let's practice with a feeling. Say your significant other has left you, and you are feeling despair. You can try to select some positive thoughts that will be able to help you to move up the Feeling States ladder. Remember, there are 10 Feeling States. You only need to move to a slightly higher feeling state. Thus, it is only necessary to select a thought that moves you slightly higher. Moving up a single level to the next, slightly more positive one is an accomplishment.

For this example, you realize that the thought you had was " I am now alone". The feeling state that you felt closest associated with you feeling alone is Frustration. For you to feel improvement it is not necessary or possible for you to shoot up to Love / Joy. Instead you need only move up one feeling state, to Contentment.

To move up to Contentment you can turn around the thought to it's positive association. This can be accomplished in many ways. For example, what could be a positive thing about being alone? You might have more time to go back and finish your education? Perhaps you can regain the sense of independence you once had. It may even now be possible for you to find your ideal partner? The idea is that you keep thinking of things until you come across thoughts that make you feel better.

Buried Rage

What is the price of nice? I can say that in my life it cost me dearly, for I developed 2 separate strivings that diametrically opposed each other. One was the good boy. The one that stayed inside the lines. He was always calm and sensitive, always eager to please. Everyone loved him, and they loved me for being such a good person.

The other side of me, my shadow side was the exact opposite. He was a risk taker and playboy. He was the secret keeper. He was totally out for himself. Often he was judge, jury, and executioner, keeping a firm leash on the do - gooder, only allowing my sensitive side out in public places.

The frequency difference between these two sides of me became greater and greater. In short, I became conflicted. My life began to be more and more out of control. First I thought I must choose one or the other. However I soon saw that this led me to resistance, because all it did was add stress and anxiety, amplifying the out of control behavior and need for control.

It wasn't until I finally understood the dynamics of energy that I realized the way to end my struggle with myself. The answer for me was LOVE. I had to love BOTH parts of myself. I had to honor both energies, for each energy had it's light side, and dark side. For example the light side of being goodness is obvious, but not so obvious is that self centered also means being self focused.

Energy does not die. It merely transforms into something else. You can not kill feelings by burying them. You can only end a feeling by resolving it. Karol Truman in her book on Feelings teaches that feelings can be altered from negative to positive. By changing the nature of our thoughts we change our beliefs. When our beliefs change, our energy changes. We create negativity when we "show bad faith", or pretend to be something that our true self is not.

The power of thought is just beginning to be understood. For example, every elementary student learns that light moves at 186,000 miles per second. Thought, however is estimated to move

700 times faster, or 130,200,000 miles per second.

Thought is energy. Energy moves in pulses similar to waves. The closeness of the waves is called its frequency. Everything has its own frequency. The tighter together the waves, the higher the frequency. The further apart the waves the lower the frequency. Positive things tend to have higher frequencies, and negative things tend to have lower frequencies. Feelings are the same way, thus people who are feeling good vibrate at high frequencies. The lower one's vibration, the more negative they tend to feel.

Chapter Eleven

The Mastery of Intention

Each moment you make a decision to be centered and whole, or not.
Each moment you create either in wholeness or not.
Each of your creative moments send out a creative force into the universe, or not.
— Barbra Brennan

Comprehending Non Locality

Non Locality has been understood by shamans and indigenous people for centuries. However it was not until developments in quantum physics that the western world has been able to prove its existence. Basically they found that when you put two particles together and then separate them, no matter how far apart you move them they will maintain influence on one another.

Somehow they become entangled with each other with a bond that still defies scientific understanding. Yet scientists observe the particles influencing each other in different locations. You may even have had the experience of knowing when a loved one needs you or is about to call, even though there can be great distances between you. These are called Non Local Events.

The understanding of the concept of Non Local Events leads us to better understand how people are influenced by other's intentions whether they are near or far away. Scientist have shown that even in our own bodies every molecule and cell constantly influences each other. Thus a change in the simplest thought, or tiniest atom through intention can influence the entire body!

Science has proven that every particle inside us is engaged in constant conversation with every other particle it has ever come into contact with. This is called Entanglement. We are entangled with everything in the universe, and everything in the universe is entangled with us. Particles that travel here from distant galaxies have been exchanging information with every other particle that it came into contact with along the way. Do you see why separation is an illusion?

This is radically changing what we thought of the vast void of space. We now know that this so called empty space is in fact teeming with living particles, which are actively exchanging information. This back and forth exchange on a sub atomic level is very minor, but when you magnify these energy exchanges over real world distances you get an unimaginably large state of energy called the Zero Point Field.

If you and I were standing just one meter apart, the particle energy exchanges in the so called empty space between us is theorized to be substantial enough to boil all the oceans of the world. Lets stop and think about that. Do you know how much heat you would need to boil an ocean? Yet they say that just one meter of space could boil ALL the oceans of the world. Multiply that by all the space on the planet, and you see the potential for those who learn to harness the energy of the universe.

The Observer Effect

We use to think that light traveled in beams. This was an illusion, because when quantum physicists developed machines advanced enough to detect it, they found that light traveled in waves. They also found that the particles seemed to exist in two places at the same time. It is now understood that particles are not like single seats in a stadium. Each particle is the entire stadium!

This is called the Observer Effect. Your reality depends on your perception. Your perception depends on where you are standing. Everything exists in relationship to every other thing. The observer effect proves that reality is malleable.

The idea that the conscious act of observation creates everything we consider real is a challenge to our prevailing perspective as a species. There is no aspect of life that will remain unchanged as a result of recognizing and living in the knowledge of this basic truth. Theories of everything come and go, however the observer effect remains fundamental to the formulation of those theories and indispensable to our understanding of the universe.

The Right Use of Intention

We have a thousand intentions every day. Unfortunately, for most people they are poorly formed and eventually fall away. By properly using the creation formula you can begin to strengthen your intentions. You begin to consciously choose thoughts that lead to happier feeling states. The feelings send out frequencies that attract things of similar frequency.

We are human antennas. If you doubt this walk over to a radio or television set in the room and try to get a better picture. The screen will get clearer when you touch it. This can only happen because you are an antenna, and just like your body can tune in tv signals it can also pick up many other signals and frequencies across time and space.

Besides being receivers we also send out energy and are also transmitters. We can now observe spikes in electrostatic charge during healing sessions from healers. This remained true whether or not the test subjects where close together or far apart. The most important factor was whether or not the subject maintained the intention of healing. Intention is vital in any equation. For without intention you have nothing, and with intention every possibility becomes instantly available!

When we learn to harness the power of intention and can wield it at will we become masters of our world. Today that possibility is available to every sentient being.

Indigenous cultures have known for centuries that thoughts create things. Western science has only recently begun to study and quantify just what intention is and how it works in the world. In the 1970's a scientist named Fritz – Albert Popp found that all living things emitted a constant current of light. He further found that the light is used to communicate between organisms.

Later scientists found that light carries information. Take for example a star. The light from a star may take millions of years to reach us. The image we get carries information with it about the star even if it long ago died.

Everything in the universe responds to everything else. Not just chemically on a quantum level, but also through light communication. We now can prove that even microscopic bacteria are in constant communication with each other even when they are not touching one another.

Plants are no different. Experiments have shown that plants respond to stimuli even when they are not in direct contact with the stimulus. One experimenter noticed that the plants he had hooked up to measuring devises registered a response to boiling water being poured down the sink. It wasn't until closer examination that they noticed the plants were actually responding to bacteria that was found in the sink drain.

This would then be replicated with shrimp and yogurt. and a host of other organisms and conditions. Researchers found that plants responded to threats of pain or death of other organisms whether they were in the room with them or miles away. The important variable seemed to be the intent of the perpetrator. Once the plant picked up the communication it reacted by a rise in electrostatic activity.

Perhaps most amazing was that they also got the same spike from the plants when someone merely THOUGHT of doing harm. When healers were studied they also were able to get corresponding spikes in the plants during healings. Clearly these type of findings point to an inter connection between all things. The results demand further inquiry so that we can learn how to harness and control these energies for the good of All That Is.

Love Is Fire

Love Is Fire
When it's fire storm is through
There's only ashes left of you

Love is transformational
Something old is laid low
But from the ashes
A rainforest will grow

Love is the unknown
Hidden in every breeze
Life's longing seed
Blows forth
And while picking roses
Sacrifice your hand to thorns

From dust the path is made
A way is found
Remember child
The road to heaven
Begins in hell

So rejoice in your mutation
Bliss pursued promises rejuvenation
You must risk it all to gain it all
You may say seize the day
But I say seize the way

My lover calls me to come dance
To step outside and take a chance
The ego must relinquish its hold
All that I built up
I now let go
I now let go......

~ Kazi Kearse

Chapter Twelve

Healing Yourself, and Your World

" DNA can be activated by radio and light waves keyed to human language frequencies...Specifically, the unity consciousness associated with unconditional love...to heal not only the mind and spirit, but the body as well"
- Sol Luckman, Author of Conscious Healing

Era III Medicine

Human evolution has had many evolutionary points in its development. Human consciousness has also been developing in an evolutionary pattern. Human systems are not steady, but instead are in a constant state of flux. Once, we traveled in clans for food. Eventually we formed societies and governments. Sometimes with very rigid rules. There is a new shift coming, as the governments, and rigid rules, breakdown and are replaced by more advanced human systems.

In the area of health and medicine Sol Lukeman has indentified 3 eras. Era I has been identified as beginning in the 1600's AD. This was the beginning of western medicine, and the mechanistic approach to healing. At this time there was a great power struggle between the Catholic Church and various governmental powers for the hearts, minds, and will of the people. Who got jurisdiction over the mind / soul, and who got control of the body became vital as scientific discoveries began to influence more and more societies.

The human body in Era I medicine is completely separate from the soul. The body is seen as purely physical, and responding to purely physical laws. The experts in these laws are the doctors. Individual experience plays no part in this model. The laws of God are understood solely by it's experts, the priests.

Era II Medicine began with the realization in the 1900's AD, of the Placebo Effect. The Placebo Effect proved that there is an inter relationship between mind and body, and that individual experience effects outcomes. The church and governments during Era II begin to lose influence in people's lives. Religion begins to be replaced with Spirituality, as a guiding force.

During Era II people find that they can remedy ills of the body by changing their thoughts. Mind – Body approaches begin to get popular. People begin to understand the power of positive thinking over the course of their illness.

The structure of the family also changes during Era II . It use to be that families in the previous era had to stay close together for survival. During Era II there is a gradual change from interdependence to intradependence. Intradependent Families are as tight knit as interdependent families. The main difference is that in interdependent families each individual is a spoke in the wheel of the family. Authority rests with the head of the family. It was very much needed at the beginning of the 1600's AD, but not as much needed by the end of the 1900's AD. By the end of Era II each individual in the family increasingly had more say in their individual destinies.

We are now at the very beginning of what is being called Era III Medicine. In Era III there is the realization that a force exists outside the individual's body that can influence its healing and personal development. Currently the force is called many different things by many different people. I call it energy or more specifically Source Energy. The influence of Energy Medicine is growing rapidly, especially as the scientific evidence builds more and more support.

While the human being is made up of this energy it also is able to manipulate the energy to preferred outcomes. Authority rests with the individual. The human mind is able to operate not only within the body but also outside the body in the individual's energy field and the multitude of greater fields in the community and greater universe. The individual is not limited to local influence only, but is able to also influence things non locally.

What Is The Light Body?

The light body is made up of energy. We all have a light body. The rate of vibration of the light is reflected in the quality and color of our light. Since everything is made up of vibrating energy, then everything has a light body and radiates light. This is as true for a rock as it is for you or me.

Science has told us that there are many spectrums of light that we do not see with our conscious minds, such as ultra violet. Because we do not see it, does not mean that it is not effecting us. We have been able to make machines that pick up these light frequencies that we cannot see. Kirlian photography has been around for awhile and is a way to photograph our light bodies.

These light bodies, or energy bodies radiate out of us and can tell a lot about us, if we are in the presence of someone who can interpret what they see. Our light bodies correspond to our degree of health and happiness. Medical Intuitives have for centuries maintained that they can see things in our energy bodies.

Within the light are light codes, and much like our DNA, it exchanges information energetically about us. While DNA codes determine what we look like, and how we feel about everything, so too do light codes. By activating certain codes through manipulation of our intentions we are able to change our reality, and what we see.

New Thought science is pouring in from around the world and turning the old science on its head! Bruce Lipton is showing through what is being called Epigenetics, that each cell of our body, and even the universe has consciousness. Epigentics also says that through thought, and intention, we can change our own DNA. So for example, if a deceased cancer cell wants to, it can regain its health, light, and vitality. Just as easily as genes turn themselves off, they can turn themselves on again.

The New Trinity (Light, Sound, Intention)

The smallest child, hiding under their blanket during a thunderstorm knows that light is accompanied by sound. The two things go together. Most of the time though, in the natural world, we are handicapped by our senses that do not perceive very much of the full light or sound spectrums. Scientist once again with their machines have stepped up and shown that light and sound travel through space for billions of years without end.

As these two forces travel through space they interact with all the other molecules and subatomic particles in their path. They in fact communicate in a language all their own (codes). Deep space radio telescopes are deciphering information about the nature of our expanding universe and the origins of the big bang.. The Hubble telescope has picked up sources of light from distant galaxies that has traveled for many billions of years.

Together sound and light are helping shape the newest theories of the universe. We know now that there is a Galactic Center in our own Milky Way Galaxy, from which we are expanding from. We know that galaxies rotate around clusters of galaxies, which in turn, rotate around super clusters of galaxies....and on and on. While all the time the universe is expanding. We also know that the rate of expansion is speeding up, instead of slowing down., which often happens in an explosion. Some theorists believe that eventually the universe will slow and begin to collapse back to center. Perhaps this is the natural cycle of the universe?

Chapter Thirteen

Developing Limitless Love

" The experience of unconditional love begins in your heart, not in someone else's. Don't make your ability to love yourself conditional on someone else's ability to love you".
- Paul Ferrini

Limitless Love

Those words set me free, when I first heard them. It was confirmation of something I have felt inside for so long, but had never given words to it. It was the exact opposite of what society tried to have me accept all these years. The fallacy that makes you pin all your hopes for love on one form, one person, who you must vow to be with for the rest of your life, regardless of what may come.

The fallacy of romantic love combines with the ego to convince us that we "have" a spouse or lover. To the Ego it actually feels like we have ownership, or claim to the object of our so called love. I say "so called love", because this is not true love.

True love is limitless. This instead is still from fear based love. When you love yourself you do not fear being alone. Being alone is an opportunity to love yourself even more! You know that love is limitless in the universe. If one person, or form loses interest in you, or rejects you, you know that the loving universe will provide more forms in the future.

End your fear! Trust in a loving universe. You are your own judge, jury, and executioner. You are also free, at any moment, to be your own redeemer. You are in a temporary world. Give up the illusion of permanence. Nothing is permanent in this world! Friends, lovers, bodies, all "things" in life pass away.

When you see your beloved in everyone, then everyone becomes your beloved. Open fearlessly to love and all its changing forms. Wanting what is best not only for yourself, but for your beloved. Even to the point if it ultimately leads to separation of the partnership. When you are grounded in your understanding that you are an eternal being you know that we are never truly separated, and no separation is eternal. You know that we come together at certain times and sometimes we go through a particular lifetime together, and other times we have other things that we must experience separately.

It is time to end the fear of freedom with those we say we love. The words " I love you, and I want to be with you, right now", becomes a beautiful phrase, and the hope in my heart that I can help you to achieve your greatest good, is my highest task. I would love for your greatest good to be with me, but I know that that may not always be the case.

No longer do I try to keep love. For when I try to keep love I realize that I have destroyed it. I enjoy my alone time, and no longer fear it. I do not need to manipulate another to keep me from feeling alone. For when I am alone I am still with my own love for myself, and that's become a really good thing! If I am rejected by someone I do not wallow in feeling unworthy. I know that I am love, and love is all around me. What should I have to fear?

The outcome is guaranteed! We are in an expanding universe and therefore we will all reach the same spot one day. We all will eventually reach enlightenment. Thus be easy on yourself. Do not strain to force yourself to go where you are not ready to go yet. For this is not about keeping up with anyone, it's about knowing yourself! Do not try and force a blissful feeling if you are not feeling it. The feeling will arrive itself, naturally, when it is the right time.

You are exactly where you should be right now. Love is all around you, if you could only see it. It is limitless, and when you are able to get in the flow with it, you can become an expression of limitless love to yourself and others. Only your beliefs can cast you out from the flow, and only your beliefs can keep you in the flow. While staying in the flow is preferable, (when we remember that we are eternal beings) we can also realize that our time in the flow will increase over time and assure us that bliss, enlightenment, and limitless love will all be permanent states for all of us eventually!

War Is Over

Love ends war. For love and war cannot exist alongside each other. When you are filled with love you cannot do violence to yourself or others. You become much more patient with yourself and others. Expanding, eternal beings do not have to be anxious over getting things done "right" all the time, nor lose sleep over imperfections.

Everyone will awaken at their own pace. Each individual will drop their conditional love patterns after they have experienced the failure of it being able to make them happy for long. Each of us come here to experience contrast, and to grow from experiencing it. Contrast is the difference you experience between what you desire to happen and what actually happens. If this planet is a school room, than contrast is the main curriculum!

When you become love you end your quarrels with those around you. Since we are all God, and all made up of the same Source Energy, in essence one being; who is it we are really fighting? You may think that you hate your neighbor, but the contrast he provides for you is vital to why you are down here, and will be what advances you, and ultimately leads to your freedom. Thus the pain they cause you is also advancing you.

We know that in the grand scheme of things, our dramas are self created, and designed to challenge and advance us. We also know that when we have disputes with people, we are really arguing with God, who is in the temporary form of our neighbor.

Time after time we have seen that this only leads to suffering. So now we may turn to our neighbor, and try reacting differently. We can act from the love inside us, and we can find the loving response.

Life is like a river. Too often we try and swim against the current. We resist what life is trying to show us. We get caught up in the forms, that life is presenting us with, instead of seeing past them. So we try and go upstream, when life is flowing downstream. We forget that love is a boat!

Any victories the globalists have are temporary. The human spirit will triumph. It's something they leave out of their equations, but it will be what ultimately brings a new day. They may control the OUTPUT (our actions), but they do not control the INPUT (our thoughts). They design grids, but there is not a grid ever made that can withstand human ingenuity, and free will. Through creativity, wisdom, love, and the pure ability to outlast them, all their cages will fail. See, for all they control, they cannot control HOW we decide to take in their information. The awakened mind is by it's nature unpredictable. A mind that rises above rewards and punishment can no longer be controlled by rewards and punishments, and yet is still getting others to also wake up. It becomes a contagion, or as I like to call it, a movement. An unstoppable force. If they are dumb enough to still choose globalism after knowing all this then I only have two words for them ... BRING IT !!!

~ Kazi Kearse "Letter To A Globalist" August, 2012

Chapter Fourteen

Reclaiming Your Sovereignty

"The Matrix is a system, Neo... But when you're inside, you look around, what do you see? Businessmen, teachers, lawyers, carpenters. The very minds of the people we are trying to save. But until we do, these people are still a part of that system... You have to understand, most of these people are not ready to be unplugged. And many of them are so injured, so hopelessly dependent on the system, that they will fight to protect it"...
-The movie " The Matrix"

The Matrix was one of the first movies that woke me up out of the corporate programmed, American dream I was put in since childhood. I had known that politically, my government had done a lot of bad things in the past. Some of them I had even protested. I knew that we were in wars that we shouldn't have been in, and corrupted or removed leaders we did not favor.

This movie was different. Although it was suppose to take place at some future time, I knew it was commenting on the world right now. I made the conscious decision to take the red pill, and I watched it over and over again, and researched some of it's themes. For those who don't know, or remember, it's about machines (Government) taking over and hooking us all up to pods from birth, that suck out our energy, while keeping us in a dream state, that everything is fine, and we are living normal lives.

By researching the government, corporations, and the history of the international bankers, I discovered that the movie is not far from the reality of what is actually going on. The owners do have us hooked up to a machine that is a vast system. From birth to death, they do want to own us, and they do live off of our energy. Just like in the movie. Except instead of having you physically hooked up to the machine, they have you psychologically, and monetarily hooked in to the system.

I'm about to discuss perhaps the scariest, most controversial topic in this book. What is really going on in the world, and how you can change your circumstances? To do this, I will discuss a very important, yet misunderstood word, Sovereignty. A Sovereign is defined as a chief, supreme, independent, or monarch.

Remember that as this chapter unwinds. You have two gifts your creator disposed on you at birth. One is sovereignty, and the other is divinity. The British Common Law that our government runs under, because we never really broke away from the crown, recognizes the difference between a sovereign and a strawman.

How You Lost Your Sovereignty

At birth you are given a name by your parents, and an entity is set aside by the government, or UNITED STATES CORPORATION (after1933) to represent you. This is called your STRAWMAN. Your name will from then on be printed in ALL CAPITAL LETTERS on all your future government documents, like birth certificate, drivers license....etc. It is only an artificial corporate person, that can be acted upon by the corporate government. Your strawman is signified by the red letters, and numbers on your birth certificate, and social security card. Your birth certificate is bought, sold, and traded on the stock exchange. Yes, the government is making money off of you! Private bankers own your strawman, and your property. The government corporation can then have the right to control the movement of you through your strawman.

A sovereign has taken back the right to their strawman and their strawman is not subject to the government's laws outside of the laws of commerce, which is the supreme law. The problem is that when your parents signed your birth certificate, or when you signed a marriage certificate, and when you paid taxes and had social security withheld...etc...You signed away your rights to sovereignty. By not objecting, you brought into reality your strawman and legally bound yourself to the rules of the UNITED STATES CORPORATION.

Your strawman is YOUR PERSON. Your person is chattel property and when the government acts upon you it acts on YOUR PERSON. It's like a coat that you can take off. If the coat is on, you must operate under the corporation's rules, for they are over you. They have the right to punish you for violating their rules. When you get the coat off, you are a sovereign, and on equal footing with the corporation (government) and cannot be punished by their laws, as long as you hold up your end of the contract, and abide by uniform commerce laws.

Along with your strawman the government corporation also creates a bond for you (the red number on your birth

184

certificate). They hold it for you and never tell you about it. They will however trade it on the stock exchange, and make money off of it.

In 1871 when congress gave the government over to the bankers, the first thing the bankers went for was the constitution. They changed the title from The Constitution for the united states of America to THE CONSTUTION OF THE UNITED STATES OF AMERICA. Why would the name change be so important to them? The answer is that now it's a corporate constitution, and the corporation is free to change it, to regulate it, and to punish person's who violate their dictates.

The DISTRICT OF COLUMBIA was set up as one of the headquarters of the corporation. This headquarters would not be under Common Law, as in the days of the old constitution, but instead the new constitution, and the new government would run under Roman Civil Law, or Admiralty / Maritime Law (Law of the Seas) also known as Private International Law.

If you haven't noticed after the bailout fiasco in 2008, congress does not work for you. Not any more. Congressmen are employees of the UNITED STATES CORPORATION. The corporation has arms called Departments. All so called "public servants" actually work for the corporation. Remember the corporation is a private, for profit entity, purely in place to serve its own interests and that of its stock holders. Thus you will find many of your local governments and police departments publicly traded on the stock market, based on how much revenue they generate for the "corporation". Now you know why there are so many traffic cops.

The days of the policeman on the corner, protecting the neighborhood are gone. They are now revenue generators for the corporation. Besides generating revenue, they also enforce the collection for it. If there are violators, they will also go after them for the corporation too. When a similar lens is held up to the court system we find the same thing. The courts work for the corporation, enforces it's laws, and punishes those who stray outside it's lines.

So how does one go about reclaiming their sovereignty? This is a matter of much debate and complication. I will not be able to fully and completely go into a detailed explanation here, however there are many places you can go for more information and to research your own answers. You can look at the video reference list link at the end of this book or on my website. The problem that I have noticed with people who go through all the trouble and relinquishments, to get rid of their strawman and become "sovereigns" is that the government still picks and chooses whether, under color of law, they care to recognize those rights. From what I have seen the government and it's enforcement arm, the police, and courts, still take what they want at gun point.

Like anything there is a full spectrum of responses to this, and each individual is free to choose their level of interest. At one end of the spectrum you have people who have moved out of their homes, resettled in the wilderness, and filed the necessary papers with the government. While at the other end of the spectrum some choose just to find out their legal rights, without ever asking the government for any redress.

For some people, their jobs, pensions, and other circumstances are too tied into the system for them to benefit from trying to remove themselves. Freedom from the UNITED STATES CORPORATION comes at a very high price, because you have been paying into the system your whole life. Perhaps by arming ourselves with this information we can better prepare our children, and future generations, so that they can live freer than we were able to?

Fighting Back

"We hold these truths to be self-evident. That all men are created equal; that they are endowed by their Creator with certain unalienable rights; that among these are life, liberty, and the pursuit of happiness; that to secure these rights, governments are instituted among men, deriving their just powers from the consent of the governed; that whenever any form of government becomes destructive of these ends, it is the right of the people to alter or abolish it, and to institute new government, laying its foundation on such principles, and organizing its powers in such form, as to them shall seem most likely to effect their safety and happiness."

— Excerpted from the Declaration of Independence of the original thirteen united states of America, July 4, 1776

If you decide you want to seek freedom legally you must first get possession of your strawman. Right now the government has responsibility for your strawman. There are two types of law / courts. Thus there are two types of jurisdiction. I will only be able to give you the briefest of outlines here.

Admiralty Law began during medieval times under King Richard The Lionheart. It is the law of the sea. It is how people did business on the high seas. It was based on Roman Civil Law. It involved presenting documents when ships came into port with supplies. This was called a birth, which is signified today by a birth certificate. This announces your docking, or arrival in the world.

This became the law of commerce (or UCC law) and it became international law, binding corporations, and people from different countries who needed a common language to do business with each other, and punish companies, or people who went outside that agreed upon arrangement.

Every ship has a captain and crew. In the United States, the president is the captain, and by law, you are the crew. The crew has no rights that the captain cannot overrule. By becoming a sovereign and gaining your sovereignty you become your own captain. There is a price to pay however, and sovereignty needs to be decided carefully, on a case by case basis, since the ocean is big, rough, and it is easy to get lost at night!

Personal Sovereignty is our birthright, however it is taken from us at birth, and it is up to us to claim it back. Each person must decide to do so individually and in your own way. Some people can make court challenges. Some people can choose to stop cooperating with the system, in the government, at work, at the bank, or whichever other places they choose.

A word of caution. These rules, and agreements are predicated on the assumption of a lawful corporate government. This unfortunately is not the case. It is quite possible that you can play their game, untangle yourself from all their corporate ties, and then find that the government really rules by force, and not by law. It is called "color of law".

I for one, believe that our government operates under color of law. I believe that when it comes down to it, the oligarchs want only serfs, and will not tolerate a lobby of freemen, anymore than they would tolerate a free country next to them. They would want to weaken it, and crush it, if given the chance.

So for now, these are the rules they put on the books. I, however have no idea whether they will honor them when more and more people begin to take their rights of sovereignty back. I am doubtful they will, because in the end, these are criminals, not honorable men and women.

Part Three:

Abundance Thinking

Chapter Fifteen

The Abundance Thinking 12 Step Program

"Oh while I live, to be the ruler of life, not a slave, to meet life as a powerful conqueror, and nothing exterior to me will ever take command of me."
- Walt Whitman

Like lucid living, Conscious Co Creating is the next level in human evolution. It is the ability to choose outcomes in your life by choosing your thoughts, feelings, and beliefs. Candace Pert, who herself has made many great scientific discoveries has said that this new age will be known not for great technological breakthroughs, but for the finding that we are creators of our own universes, and that thought determines our physical world.

Begin by keeping a journal. Write down your thoughts when you awaken in your waking, and non waking dreams. Walk between the two worlds. Pay attention to the words you use. How do you label things? What do you create by what you say? How do others treat you? Do you choose love or fear?

Although we have run from it most our lives, love is what feels right. We can create more love in our life by choosing it more, and making that choice more often throughout our day, and night. When we lucidly come across choices between love and fear, and we consciously choose love, we are on our way to creating a higher vibration. The more we do this, the stronger our vibration becomes, and we begin attracting new things to us based upon our repeated beliefs.

On Love

I will not try and tell you one way to love. As conscious co creators you can each find your own way to love. For some it will be through partnership, for others you may find your bliss on the open road. Remember, you are eternal beings, and have each benefited from the rewards of many varied combinations over your many lifetimes.

The key I think, is to always try and do what would be the loving response to do, and to always stay true to your self. So do not accept another's desire, or picture of love, in place of your own. Always follow your own inner guidance to what feels better.

Sacred Relationships are possible. They require the mutual understanding that each person's first relationship is with their self. The couple can then work as partners knowing that they will each be the teacher of the other person. They also understand that there are always 3 entities in any relationship; me, you, and us.

I am responsible for me, in everyway possible, and I do not expect anyone to take any responsibility for or from me. You are responsible for you. I will not seek to invade, usurp, or otherwise take for you, your responsibility. We, are responsible for us. The relationship's success or failure is not to be blamed on one person. Both people must put into defining the relationship.

Each partner learns to give each other the freedom to follow their own soul's calling. Each partner challenges each other to do the work that they need most to do. We are perfect teachers for each other. We help each other not go back to sleep. The nature of a true partnership is based on mutual respect and the understanding that "no tree has branches so foolish as to fight amongst themselves".

While we can enjoy the "us" of a relationship, at the same time we must never get lost in the "us" of the relationship. We must cultivate our own voice. What is right for one may not be right for both. We need to become independent of the good opinion of others.

On Money

I will not tell you that there is one kind of right livelihood. For you can find freedom through all professions. Your freedom may come from finally connecting with the source of abundance in the universe, that money freely flows from, or your freedom may come from relinquishing the need for financial gain. Money is not the end point, it is only a tool.

Money can be a tool to open you to your full possibilities. I believe that the lack of money is currently being used by God, or Source, to open people spiritually. To flush out spiritual strengths that would have normally gone untouched. It is a tool of quickening, that is being chosen by more and more souls.

Is it hard to believe that you would purposely do this to yourself? As I have said many times in this book, remember you are eternal beings. Your entire life is but a day's school lesson, from the place of your soul. Perhaps however, your lesson in today's class is how to consciously choose abundance? Perhaps if you focus your thoughts on abundance more and more, money will begin to flow to you? Soon your predominant thought could be that "money flows to me, easily, and abundantly"!

It is very important that you connect to your source daily. Light your fire of being daily, and feel its glowing power expand, filling you and your world with love. Remember this is an abundant universe, and you have more than enough universal creation energy at your disposal. You have all that you need at your disposal, and more than enough for any task your soul has chosen.

Do not fall back into your victim mode. Always remember that you have chosen this, and that you are co creating with All That Is. I can remember that there was a time in my life when I felt devoid of love in my life. I asked God to bring love into my life, no matter how hard it was going to be, or what form it would take.

The good news was that it worked. The universe began to slowly flood me with friends who brought tremendous love into my life. Events came to me in my life, increasing the love vibration that was growing in me. My connection to the universe deepened. In fact this book is the result of me asking that one question.

Yet I want you to understand that there is a flip side to this asking, and manifesting. For many people, including myself, you have to go through hell to get to heaven! For your request for change often means that your old world must be wiped away. Sometimes the very things in your life that you counted on will be removed from you.

During these times it will be important to remember your role, or job. Your job is to ask. The universe's job is to bring it to you. You cannot judge the form it is brought to you in. It might be very different than you imagined. For example you may ask for love and find that the universe brings you a new person to love in your life, but also brings you a divorce, and you lose the house you've worked for, and the family unit you were accustomed to.

This underscores the need for really putting thought into what you decide to ask the universe for. Source Energy does not debate whether what you are wanting is good or bad. Those judgments mean little to eternal beings anyway. It is only concerned with attracting more of what is being put out there.

I have come up with the following affirmation. You can use it as it is, or change it to suit your personal wantings:

Daily Affirmation

"I release all that I was

And open myself to all that I am.

Connecting with the flow of love I am.

I know that I have within me all I desire.

The universe calls it forth out of me

And into my world to make manifest.

I believe absolutely in my strength, connection,

And oneness with All That Is".

- Kazi Kearse

The Science of Getting Rich

There is a science to getting rich. By this I mean that there are certain laws in the universe, such as the law of attraction, that each of us can learn to harness, and create anything we want in our life. I owe much of my understanding of these laws of financial abundance to Wallace D. Wattles.

I need to preface the following, because some of you will have great difficulty with the notion of getting rich. Ever since we were little children we were taught not to be greedy or want for too much riches, as the pursuit of money was sinful.

Yet we live in an abundant universe. God wants us to find greater and greater expressions of greatness in his name. Life calls to us to be all that we can be. Our minds expand with creativity pushing us ever onward. This is the nature of the advancing man.

To this end, man must have the greatest access possible to his / her physical, mental, and spiritual development. This is an inalienable right we receive at birth. We have a right to be all that we can be, and to this end, requires vast sums of money in today's modern society. The cost of living continues to climb. Whether you are talking about gas prices, housing costs, taxes....etc. To be the full creator that you were born to be you will need to allow the universe to bring you the vast sums of money that will be required.

Key to understanding how to create wealth is understanding that there is one substance in the universe. Wallace D. Wattles called it " Thinking Substance", many today call it Source Energy. It is everywhere and in everything. When we think a thought in this substance, an image of the thought is created, and that item is delivered to us through other people, and events that are drawn to us.

While you are creating your desire it is important that you act now in a "certain way". It is important that you hold a clear mental picture of what you are wanting while you are actively pursuing the thing that you are wanting. You must maintain positive thoughts about what you want to create. Do not let any doubts in. The thing that you think about most will be created.

You will also need to have unwavering faith that you will receive what you are wanting, that it is being delivered to you right now, and that you act as though you already have it. If you can do this it is law that what you are wanting will show up in your life.

These riches will not be delivered on a magic carpet. They will be brought to you by people, and events drawn into relationship with you. You must offer more in what Wattles termed Use Value than you get in Cash Value. By Use Value, he meant how much the use of something is worth. For example, if I am selling a book I get the cash value from the reader and the reader is given use value. Thus the universe will increasingly deliver wealth to me. However if I was selling a book with junk written inside, and the reader received no use value, I would not receive the cash value from the universe.

Key to advancement will be your ability to tap into the stream of increase. This is the vibration you give off that you are an advancing individual. Wattles called these people "advancing men". These people convey that their path is always advancing upward, and they are continually offering win win situations to others. This can also apply to "advancing women".

You must maintain sincere gratitude and faith for all that will come to you. In fact you must act as if you already have the item. The more you can picture what you want, the faster it will manifest. You must hold a positive image in your mind unflinchingly. Know that it will come to you!

Focus on what you want, and put completely out of your mind what you do not want. Too many people waste their time and energy in trying to avoid what it is they do not want. Do not take your time up with thoughts of absence. By thinking about the lack of something in your life, you are maintaining its vibration, instead of developing the higher vibration you are seeking.

Thoughts of "I don't want to be poor anymore" will bring you more being "poor". Thoughts of I no longer want to do dumb things, will cause you to keep doing dumb things. For if you believe it, you will see it in your life. It's a universal law, and the universe does not judge whether it is something good or bad.

We advance by thoughts of INCREASE, and decline by thoughts of ABSENCE. Absence is an illusion. There is no source of darkness in the universe. There is only degrees of the lack of light. For light is energy, and energy is everywhere. There is nothing in the universe that is not energy.

Muscle Testing has shown consistently that untrue thoughts make muscles go weak. While true thoughts, especially positive thoughts make muscles test strong. When this scenario gets played out with each thought, thousands of times a day, it is easy to see how sickness, and disease can take hold in the body, and how choosing better thoughts can create health.

What is perhaps even more fascinating is that this happens even in non humans. Animals and even plants also test negatively, or positively according to the thoughts that are around them. In fact, in the most bizarre and most famous study, Matsu Emoto studied the response of water molecules to different thoughts focused on them and found that the water molecules took on the characteristics of the thoughts around them. Water molecules in negative thought environments were malformed, while ones that were in more positive thought environments were better formed and stronger.

Re-Scripting

A script is the subconscious language that holds our thoughts, feelings, and beliefs in place. To Consciously Co Create we need to choose which scripts we will accept and which we wish to change. The importance of changing your subconscious scripts cannot be underscored enough. The daily affirmation is a general tonic that softens old scripts. The scripts we choose to use through out the rest of the day will be what shapes our new vibration, and determines our present frequency.

Changing scripts is called Re-Scripting.. It begins by taping into the flow of Source Energy that contains every thought that was ever thought, every emotion ever felt, and every belief ever lived. For we know that energy never dies. As you quite your mind notice what frequency you are tuning in. Use one of the 10 Feeling States that most closely fits your current feelings.

After you have selected your current feeling state decide which feeling state you wish to go to. It is suggested that you choose one feeling state higher than your present feeling state. Remember, you only have access to feelings that are in vibrational alignment with your current thoughts.

Assume the feeling of the wish fulfilled. Act as if what you want is already happening. The more you can do this, and the deeper you can go with it, the faster your outer world will reflect your inner world. If you are getting stuck in feelings of lack, you simply "turn it around". Turn – Arounds are the opposite of the feelings, thoughts, and beliefs that are getting us stuck in negative vibrations. Some examples follow:

Thought / Feeling / Belief	Turn – Around
"I don't belong"	" I do belong."
	I choose being a part of All That Is. I can joyously bring myself into alignment with everything around me".
"I am bad"	" I am good."
	I am God's love in physical form". " I feel loved by All That Is".
"I am a failure"	"I am a success"
	" I choose to surround myself with success, and because I am a success magnet, successful situations come to me effortlessly".

Abraham teaches a wonderful process for finding higher thoughts. You begin by saying "wouldn't it be nice if….." in front of what it is you want. So if you have a spouse who is mistreating you and you are feeling like a failure, you can apply this process, turn around the thought by saying " wouldn't it be nice to feel loved by all that is".

By writing down our thoughts and feelings we amplify them. Thus if we record or write down our turn arounds we increase their effect. In one study, **80%** of the people who just simply wrote down in their book what they wanted, found that a year later, they had what they had written they wanted a year before. That's an **80%** likelihood that if you do the above you will receive that which you are asking for.

Getting a journal or otherwise documenting your thoughts and discoveries is crucial to becoming a creator. Modern day journalers may prefer a computer or laptop. Either way the process is the same. Feel it, and if it's negative, turn it around into a more positive thought, and write it down.

The New I Statement

I statements are a way to show that you claim your responsibility and understanding of your thought, feeling, or action; when talking with another person. It also lets the other person know that you are not claiming sole understanding of what happened, and are merely describing your interpretation of it.

Today we are ready for the next level in I Statements. Now when we wish to discuss something that the other person said or did we can say " I heard/ saw _____ and I felt

_____ ". An example would be:

"I heard your comment about me. I felt angry that you would say that about me."

Always begin with saying "I" first. Saying "You" takes away your responsibility, and usually puts the other person on the defensive. Nobody can argue with you if you stick to saying "I", because you are merely describing your own experience, and who knows better than you what you were thinking and feeling!

You Are Your Primary Relationship

When you fall in love with yourself you need nothing else to complete you. You are the cake, and everyone else is your delicious icing! It is not selfish to think like this because everyone in your life has their own scrumptious cake to make also. You cannot make it for them, and you cannot give them yours.

You are the one that you have been waiting for! This is true in love relationships, or spiritual beliefs. In the old world we needed another person to complete us. We were constantly pressured to marry by a certain age, and achieve a certain level of financial freedom. Next came the house we were expected to acquire, and 2.5 children we were to raise. All this we were suppose to put before us, and our own needs.

One day after acquiring all these things I decided to include me. I began to put me first. The people in my life at the time thought I was being selfish. They got angry with me, and began attacking me. I stood my ground, and maintained my vision. All along I tried to show them the benefits of being your own primary relationship, but all they could see was what they needed from me, and the fact that I was no longer providing it to them.

There is a new age dawning, but not everyone is going to see it at the same time. Some will cling to the old ways because it is all they knew. Others, however will welcome this new time, and all the opportunities that come with it.

Bringing your life into alignment does not mean disregarding everyone else's needs. It simply means that by making decisions that bring yourself into happiness, and joy, you are able to bring a whole person into all your relationships. That is all that anyone could ask, and your only responsibility. For if each person does this the entire group benefits with greater love, peace, and functioning.

The 5 Fundamentals

1. You are an eternal being.
2. You and everything around you is energy.
3. You will be given a body. Learn to love it, and take good care of it, for it will be from this body that you will create your world.
4. You will develop lessons for yourself. Lessons will be repeated until learned.
5. Learning does not end.

The Abundance Thinking 12 Step Principles

Step One:
I fully and completely accept that I am the creator of my universe.

Step Two:
I lay to rest the life that was planned for me in my ignorance and freely choose to follow the life I am creating with the universe.

Step Three:
I make a decision to turn my life over fully to my greatest good. I realize that the brighter my light is allowed to be, the easier it is for others around me to find their own way.

Step Four:
I make a searching and fearless inventory of my true wants, and desires. I do this without judgment or accepting anyone else's morals in place of my own. I know that there is nothing that I cannot be, do, or have.

Step Five:
I admit to myself, and at least one other person, which of the fear based feeling states I habitually get stuck in, and allow the universe to call me towards more loving ones.

Step Six:
I am ready to be one with the universe and all those around me. I accept the responsibility and joy of being both a participant and co creator in the divine manifestation of all that is.

Step Seven:
I am one with all that is. The universe flows through and around me, and I physically feel it divinely manifesting.

Step Eight:
I make a list of the actions I am taking to manifest all that I can be, do, or have.

Step Nine:
I take direct action on each unfolding of my desires. I realize that each fulfillment of a desire will give birth to another new desire.

Step Ten:
I lovingly create the world around me. I do not get stuck in feelings of lack. When I come upon them now I simply and completely choose a more loving thought for myself.

Step Eleven:
Through prayer and meditation I seek to improve my conscious contact with God as I understand God, praying only for knowledge of my path.

Step Twelve:
Through having a spiritual awakening I carry my message to others and try to practice these principles in all my thoughts and deeds.

The 12 Steps In Detail:

Step One:

" I fully and completely accept that I am the creator of my universe".

This 12 Step program is based on the 12 Step format used successfully to help many people regain conscious control over their lives. The first step for any addict is to admit that they are an addict. The majority of the population is addicted to one thing or another. While many people find help in 12 Step programs, they concentrate all too much on "lack". Much of the person's energy is focused on what they are trying not to do anymore (ie…drinking, drugs, food, …etc.).

So in this program the focus is on the positive thoughts, feelings, and activities of someone who is being the conscious creator in their life. The only addiction that we have is our attachment to the pain body, and our attachment to the social emotional environment we grew up with. It's an addiction that each and every one of us deals with day in and day out.

The first principle affirms that you understand that YOU accept that YOU are the creator of YOUR universe. You stand up and take the responsibility for your own happiness, or your own despair. Your own abundance, or your own poverty. You no longer allow yourself the illusion that it's because of where you were born, or what someone did, or didn't do to you.

Sure, you recognize that these things happened to you, but you also recognize that they made you who you are today! You remember that this is the earth school. If you did not take those lessons you would not be who you are today. You would be something else, someone else, and that's just not acceptable, because you love yourself deeply, exactly as you are.

Diversity is great. I'm proud of my race. While I also recognize that I am a universal soul. While I am a student of history I do not let his – story distract me from my story. My story is about abundant love, wealth, and good health. In my story I am part of a planetary awakening and everything I desire is coming to me, and when it comes to me it spurs new desires. And guess what? They are coming to me too!

For I know now that I am the creator of what I see. So even in the middle of a battle field I can choose to look at the death around me, and the invaders approaching, or I could keep my focus on the beauty of the children I could keep from harm, or put my focus on helping the injured. The choice is ALWAYS mine. See, others can create war, but only I can accept it in me. Even if the world accepted peace tomorrow, but I did not have it in me, it would be useless to me.

Step Two:

"I lay to rest the life that was planned for me in my ignorance and freely choose to follow the life I am creating with the universe".

We all individually grow up with a certain set of family and social environmental factors. They influenced who we are, however they do not have to influence who we will be, unless we consciously choose to let them. Somewhere along the lines we gave up our power to someone else. Perhaps they were bigger than us? Perhaps we feared their wrath? Perhaps we sort their safety? Often we plan one plan on top of the other, down a path we falsely feel will gain us security, or happiness. Later we see that it was an illusion.

A creator drops the story they planned while they were still under the illusion of lack. For now you are creating a new one based on freedom, and choice. You know that there is nothing you cannot be, do, or have. You know, as sure as the nose on your face, that it is also coming to you, and is just outside your door. A creator is a magnet for their desires, and because of the universal law of attraction the desires have no choice but to come to them!

We are all creating our universes. Some people for the better, some for the worse. We can create lives that are nightmares, or we can create a live of love, The choice is ours. Sometimes this is a conscious choice, and sometimes it is a subconscious choice.

Step Three:

I make a decision to turn my life over fully to my greatest good. I realize that the brighter my light is allowed to be, the easier it is for others around me to find their own way.

A conscious creator has decided to turn his/her life over to their greatest good. The ultimate litmus test for a creator is, does what they are seeking at the moment stay in line with their highest ideals. Each creator's greatest good may vary. For some it may be to give and receive love unconditionally. For others it might be to live abundantly.

They understand that when they are in alignment with their greatest good they will be able to be of the most service to themselves and others. For we are all watching each other, on many different levels. When our light shines it acts as a beacon to guide others. The brighter we shine our light, the easier it is for others to find their way out of their own darkness.

Since we are all one being, when you find your way out of the darkness it lights a way for me to do the same. When I do the same, we both are uplifted. Both of our light grows! Before long we are out of the darkness and on our way home.

Step Four:

I make a searching and fearless inventory of my true wants, and desires. I do this without judgment or accepting anyone else's morals in place of my own. I know that there is nothing that I cannot be, do, or have.

We have total freedom. Our only limit is what we believe. For if you ask for something and expect it to come, the universe will deliver it to you! There is nothing that you cannot be, do, or have. We live in an abundant universe, but we misperceive it as being limiting. We focus on all the things we lack. The glass ceiling at work, the boy friend that won't commit, the rent that's due…etc.

Think what a wonderfully supportive world it really is. Remember that Source holds super clusters of galaxies together, spins us around our sun regularly every year to the second, and even causes each blade of grass to grow evenly with its neighbor. We are all part of this magnificent dance, and don't think for a minute that you are alone, or that there is not help beyond your wildest dreams available to you.

All you need to do is begin by making an inventory of what exactly it is you are wanting. The keyword here is YOU, because you can only get into alignment with something that you are vibrating with currently. For example, you cannot get into alignment with Love, if you are vibrating at the level of Hate. The most you would be able to do is move your self up the Feeling Scale from Hate to Revenge. For revenge is actually a slightly higher vibration than hatred. Thus moving from hatred to revenge is actually a healthy step.

It is important to reflect here, that your wantings be your own. You are the creator of your universe. If you try and fit into someone else's definition of something, you will inevitably fail. Remember, thoughts become things. When your thoughts are a vibrational match with love, you will experience that. However if they are a vibrational match with fear, then you will only see fearful situations come up in your life.

Step Five:

I admit to myself, and at least one other person, which of the fear based feeling states I habitually get stuck in, and allow the universe to call me towards more loving ones.

Through my work with Abraham's teaching, I have identified 10 Feeling States, which I described earlier in the book. A Feeling State is an emotion that we feel persistently, and strongly. There are hundreds of different emotions, but I have grouped them together into 10 groups. The idea is to move up this ladder of Feeling States one at a time. There is no need to jump ahead or to remain stuck.

Once you have felt which of these states you are at you can begin to consciously move your Emotional Feeling State higher. You can do this by "deliberately intending".

By deliberately intending you choose a thought that belongs to an Emotional Feeling State that is slightly higher than the one you are on.

So for example, if you are currently on Emotional Feeling State # 8 Revenge, because you have been physically abused by your husband, for a very long time, and you feel consumed with thoughts that you want to get him back. You can deliberately intend, and consciously choose a slightly higher thought such as "I am angry with you", but without the need to seek out revenge.

Another example is going from the need to blame somebody for doing something hurtful to you, to being able to just allow the frustration, and pain, without attaching blame to it. I found it such a relief when I learned that I could do this. I would now be the one in control of my feelings!

Once I learned this I now had the power of manifestation. I was manifesting thoughts, and you can do this too. By holding focus on a thought we manifest a feeling, by holding focus on a feeling we manifest an Emotional Feeling State, by focusing on a Emotional Feeling State we shape our physical reality. To shape our physical reality we need to practice this Manifestation Focusing as much as possible. Start by practicing holding a single thought in focus.

Choose something that you would like to manifest in your life. Visualize it intensely. What does it look like, smell like, feel like…etc? Feel like you really have it right now. If you can, vocalize it out loud. Speak as if you have it already. Have fun, and see what happens next.

Some things may appear shortly, and some things may take repeated focusing. If you focus 10 times consciously on being worthy, but unconsciously focusing 1000 times that day on not being worthy, then you can see that your progress will be slow...But if you increase your worthy thoughts to 100 times a day, and decrease your unworthy thoughts to 10 times a day, then you stand a much better chance of vibrationally bringing the request to you, since each thought is vibrationally attracting things of like vibration to it.

Step Six:

I am ready to be one with the universe and all those around me. I accept the responsibility and joy of being both a participant and co creator in the divine manifestation of all that is.

When we learn how to manifest we realize the duality of the immense power we hold and the shear minuteness that our individual personality holds in All That Is. For as we come closer to fully understanding that we are one with everything, our individual self begins to disappear, and we begin to glimpse ourselves as part of a singularity, that I have come to know as "All That Is". It goes by many names, God, Source Energy...etc. All these names represent the same thing.

There is also another type of duality to comprehend. There is a great responsibility to manifest the appropriate things into our lives. For we are husbands, daughters, and neighbors to many other souls. All who are equally deserving of fulfilling their wantings. Sometimes our desires will match those around us, and other times they will cause friction, even opposition in others. Such is the pain, but also the juice of life!

How can the immense ocean that is life contain so much? Is All That Is so vast that it contains all wantings? What will be your place in it? Are you ready to consciously co create? You've been unconsciously co creating all your life. Think of how wonderful it will be to choose what you want in life.

Step Seven:

"I am one with All That Is. The universe flows through and around me, and I physically feel it divinely manifesting".

I am one in thought, and action with the universe. I have learned how to flow with it and to perceive its flow through me. I do not mean this figuratively. I mean you can actually feel universal energy flowing through the palm of your hand. If you sit still you can also feel it flow around you, and right through you.

You can begin to feel it by placing your hands in front of you. Leave about 3 – 6 inches between your two hands. Slowly begin moving them, further apart, and then back towards each other, and then further apart, and closer together again. Continue this slow movement until you begin to feel something between your hands. To some of you it will feel like a force, or ball of energy. To other people it will feel like a sensation such as heat, or a tingle.

Practice this daily, until you begin to feel it more and more. This is the force that moves the big and small through out All That Is. Mastery of this step will allow you to manipulate energy, thus manipulating your manifestations. You can also heal with this power. Both yourself, and another. It is also possible for gatherings of creators to send energy to others, regardless of distance, or even time/space.

Soon you come to see All That Is, is divinely manifesting. You see that not only you are manifesting perfectly for now, but so is the planet, and the cosmos…etc. This realization comes to you despite the outward realities of war, disease, and famine that you may see around you, or in the news.

You remember that we are eternal beings, eternally manifesting. We are forever increasing our vibration of light and source energy. Do not fear your present situation for it is transitory. Remember that by choosing a different thought you change your bio-chemical makeup, and the quality of energy you are emitting and working with. That energy will attract people and situations to you that are of like vibration.

Thus you can change any situation you find yourself in. By choosing a more loving thought you will divinely manifest the people, places, and things in your life that you have been desiring. The key is to maintain that vibration so that it becomes your dominant vibration.

Step Eight:

"I make a list of the actions I am taking to manifest all that I can be, do, or have".

This step is pretty straight forward. You start by creating a list of actions you are taking to manifest all the things you desire. You are free to choose anything that you want to be, do, or have. Remember that thoughts become things. Be sure to choose thoughts, and actions that are towards your greatest good. Get rid of judgments about your worthiness or ability to attain these goals. For now, all you have to do is think the thought, or desire. That is your job. The job of the universe is to bring the people, places, and things to you.

Step Nine:

I take direct action on each unfolding of my desires. I realize that each fulfillment of a desire will give birth to another new desire.

As your chosen thoughts begin to manifest things into your life you will have the opportunity to choose new thoughts that are of similar or even higher frequency. If the thought is of a positive nature, you will continue to attract positive things. If the thought is of a negative nature, or lack, you will only attract negative things to you. Thus thoughts need to be chosen carefully.

What do you do with a negative thought? It is important not to try to stop a negative thought by force. No amount of will power can change a thought of lack. The only way to change it is by thinking a new thought that is of a higher frequency.

Keep in mind, that there is no source of evil, or darkness in the universe, there is only areas of lesser light. Everything is from the same Source. Things just vibrate at different frequencies. There are low frequencies, and high frequencies.

Your job is to continue to choose thoughts that are of higher and higher vibrations. Each fulfillment of a desire will give birth to a new desire. For example, you may desire to make $200,000 and have all that that brings, and once you've done that you may desire to make $1 million and have all that that brings.....etc.

Step Ten:

I lovingly create the world around me. I do not get stuck in feelings of lack. When I come upon them now, I simply and completely choose a more loving thought for myself.

Love is the prime directive. I do not mean the pie in the sky, always nice kind of love. Sometimes love is not kind. At least not on the surface, or to the person experiencing it. A loving reaction is sometimes letting go. So love can be a divorce, or even malignant cancer. For they are just transitions from one reality, into another. We can hold tight to the life we know, or smile as we let it go, and witness the new becoming.

If you can maintain love in your thoughts your inner and outer world will begin to reflect it. It will not matter to you as much what others around you are choosing to create in their world. For you know we are all eternal beings, lovingly co creating. The world around you at the moment can be calm, or chaotic. This will have little effect on you, because you are manifesting light from your own stream. You can be in a chaotic world, but you will only see the light.

The opposite is also true. Someone can be surrounded by love and not see it. In their world they see themselves as always being a victim. They are always lacking something. Lacking love, lacking money, lacking health....etc. The list of lacks can be endless, and as long as they are in their mind, lacking something, they will continue to attract more of that.

Understanding the 10 Feeling States is key here. Every thought that you choose has a frequency somewhere in one of the ten Feeling States. So if you find yourself thinking how you would like to pull someone's hair out one root at a time, you might identify that as a thought corresponding with the Revenge feeling state. You can then choose a new thought to plant in it's place. For example thinking a thought like I am still angry with them but I release my feelings of revenge and ask the universe to send them guidance, would be a step up in frequency, because I would be going from the feeling state of Revenge to the feeling state of Anger. The ultimate goal is to be able to send the person pure love, from a State of Joy, but we often have to crawl our way up the feeling scale.

Step Eleven:

Through prayer and meditation I seek to improve my conscious contact with God as I understand God, praying only for knowledge of my path.

You will need to maintain a regular prayer or meditation practice. This will allow you to keep a constant line of communication going between your personality and your soul. You are a tri-part being. You are made up of body, mind, and soul. All 3 units need to be properly communicating with each other for you to function healthily.

Your body reflects the quality of the thoughts you think. By properly meditating you are able to seek further clarity on fulfilling your desires. Your ancestors are waiting and willing to guide you. You are healing them when you are healing yourself. Each time you clear an issue that has blocked your light you will be clearing it for 7 generations backwards, and 7 generations forward.

Thus you can see that the universe loves and supports your every effort. So you not only change a pattern that affected your children, but you also heal it for your children's children. You are such a lovely creator. Time after time my ancestors thank me for my efforts and aide me in deepening my communication with them.

Step Twelve:

Through having a spiritual awakening I carry my message to others and try to practice these principles in all my thoughts and deeds.

As your vibration increases and you become better, and better at attracting positive things into your life, you will be given a spiritual crisis to overcome. If you maintain your focus, strength, and integrity you will come out the other side, being reborn spiritually. However, if you retreat and do not transmute what you are working on, than you will repeat the lesson over again.

After all, is this not the earth school? We have come here to alchemically turn vibrations into physical things that our soul is wishing to manifest. For we can only love others to the level of love, we love ourselves at.

The spiritual awakening of discovering who we really are, and loving and supporting that, is the true test of spirituality. The greatest spiritual task is "Know Thyself". Since time began seekers have sought spiritual experiences. Many have sought them without having gone through the dark night of the soul. It used to not be possible to avoid having to go through dark places. However now because of the new age we are in, spiritual awakening is not so far away.

Spiritual awakening is now available to those who ask for it. Do not be mistaken and think that this is easy, for it is not. You are still required to do the work, however you are not expected to go to a monastery on a mountaintop to find enlightenment. That work has already been done by our ancestors.

It is believed that the reason people are waking up in larger and larger numbers is because of those who did the work before us were vibrating at a higher level. Thus this new vibration we hold as a planet no longer requires us to do a long pilgrimage and renounce our worldly possessions.

Today, to have a spiritual experience we need to just sincerely ask for it. We then only need to wait for it, remembering to be careful not to block its return. If we can hold that vibration, of what we wanted, then we will attract it, and the universe will deliver it to us. Once it's delivered to you, you then can generate a vibration that is of an even higher caliber.

We need to get rid of the idea of some ultimate state of enlightenment that leaves us in some permanent state of having every wish fulfilled. For as we attain something that we have been wanting, we begin to seek a new wanting, and the universe sets off on bringing that to us. It never ends, nor should it. Wanting leads to experiences and experiences lead to new wantings!

Chapter Sixteen

The F-R-E-E-D-O-M Principles

Our destruction will not come from a foreign foe...but from the inattention of the people....I fear they may put too implicit a confidence in their public servants, and fail to properly scrutinize their conduct. That in this way, they may be made the dupes of designing men, and become the instruments of their own undoing. Make them intelligent, and they will be vigilant. Give them the means of detecting the wrong, and they will supply the remedy...

- *Daniel Webster*

My aim in writing this book is to aid in bolstering your knowledge, and through the information I give out to you; supply you with the remedy. To this end I have developed a psychology of freedom. Not only is it important to learn each of these principles, but it is even more important that you live them in your life.

Many people have asked me what can they do about the New World Order. I came up with the following principles so that you may have an easy to remember strategy that you can use through out your life:

The FREEDOM Principles

F ight back against the New World Order.

R esist the tyranny of the elite.

E ducate yourself and others.

E scape the matrix you were born into.

D ivest from the corporate state.

O vercome feeling helpless.

M anifest your dreams and desires.

I believe it is best to practice the freedom principles with other people, in groups, however, they can also be practiced individually. Perhaps, even individually, after you have learned them, you can seek out others, who are also learning the principles, and bringing them into their lives.

I recommend people form Abundance Circles. This can be a group of people who commit to working on the principles together, and also helping each other deal with the daily struggles of resisting the new world order. You can visit my website at the back of the book for more information on an Abundance Group you might be interested in joining, or starting.

Fight back against the New World Order

What is the New World Order? By this point in the book you have seen for yourself that it is a generalized term for a multi level plan to aggrandize a small group of people with a majority of the world's wealth and power. To achieve their ends they have corrupted our politicians, court system, military, corporations, medical, and governmental agencies.

They plan to achieve these ends by way of setting up a world government, thereby centralizing power. It is easier for a small group of (very wealthy) people to control the direction of the rest of us by setting up this control grid. Also, by centralizing their control they also centralize the profits. Meaning all the money flows to them. It is a pyramid scheme where there are only four classes of people.

The New World Order:

Aristocracy
Politicians / Media/ CEO's
Police / Lawyers / Judges/ Corporate Men
Serfs: The Lower and Middle Classes Of People

At the top of the pyramid are the Aristocracy. These will be the 13 major banking families, as well as the local despotic elite in each country, and their heirs. They will number a few thousand and be above the draconian laws that will be in place to control the masses and to funnel wealth up to them. They will have full access to underground bases and camps as well as in space. Mandatory laws will not apply to them. Technological access will be high, as will be their access to healthcare.

Just below them will be their henchmen: the politicians, media mouthpieces, and corporate CEO's, who run the businesses that churn the gears of the machine. They will taste some of the access, and some of the power of the aristocracy, but without the permanence. Though they will be paid well, and some amass great sums of money, they never escape the fact that they are an employee, and that the real money is not funneled up to them in any permanent way.

Below them are the grunts for the machine. People who have sold their soul to do the bidding for the elite. They will be in various stages of realization of what their true role is. In their minds they will be desperately trying to support themselves, and their families to remain just above serfdom. There will need to be many thousands of these people to support a worldwide government. Their pay and compensations will be adequate to maintain a minimally decent standard of living.

At the bottom will be the serfs, or average person. They will be the service workers, clerks, teachers, mechanics, and other various laborers. They will be debt slaves, if not out and out slaves. Some may be in prison or work camps due to their debt and inability to pay taxes. They will not be paid much if anything. Aristocracies see them as expendable and care very little for their happiness, after all, for a serf, there is no other choice except death.

The goal of the planners of this pyramid / New World Order is to create an efficient money making machine for themselves, that funnels all the world's profits to them in the most efficient way possible. Also in a way that is self sustainable. This idea of sustainability is key. They believe that the optimum level for this will be to only have 500 million people on the planet. Thus they have called for and begun what they are calling "The Great Culling".

That will mean the mass extinction of 7 billion people. Too much for any one war, or event. Instead they have decided to "soft kill", or slowly kill people over time, by gradually weakening people's immune systems. When people's immune systems are gone you can kill them with the slightest cold germ, and be held blameless. In fact they will say that the people did it to themselves by allowing use of toxic chemicals over a long period of time. The perfect crime.

In an effort to reach a "sustainable" or controllable population level they have poisoned your air, your food, and through vaccinations, the very blood inside your body.

I do not make these charges lightly and we will examine each of these charges in this section.

Chemtrails are chemical trails sprayed by airplanes. Mainstream media likes to say this is a conspiracy theory, however people have tested the material coming out of these planes, and have found high levels of barium (used in rat poison). Barium also effects the nervous system and is known to be lethal at high doses. When it collects in the lungs it can cause Baritosis. Baritosis is a lung problem whose symptoms are coughing, wheezing, and nasal irritation. Is it a coincidence that rates of all three of these symptoms are skyrocketing? Pardon the pun.

GMO's are Genetically Modified Organisms. They are seeds, food additives, and biological cells that are altered in a laboratory. In general they allow food growers to grow more of something at a cheaper cost. The trade for that is the destruction of our health, and every other living thing on the food chain. Obviously the price is too high, yet the companies that make GMO's are trying to pass laws that will make it illegal to grow anything that is not from GMO's.

Codex Alimentarius is a committee formed by the UN in the 1960's to regulate international standards on food production. That was its official duty, however like many UN / Rothschild schemes, there was an ulterior motive. Their true goal is to benefit large corporations, obliterate small farmers, and regulate in the secret agenda of the world government. It's been quite successful over the last four or more decades at killing small farmers, small corporations, and is poised for final victory. The criminalization of growing your own food!

There is an even more sinister part of this plan. It has to do with population control. By controlling the population of people through the food that you give them, you can make them increasingly sicker, and you can also control through targeted genetic manipulation, which populations of people ultimately live or die.

Einstein has said that when the bee's die, within 5 years, the people of the earth will die too. Well, the bees are dying. It is believed to be related to the GMO pesticides, and food that is made unnaturally in a test tube. These GMO's allow for what is called soft kill. You can kill everybody if you just do it slow enough. Most people will not even realize they are dying until it's too late. The key is to destroy the immune system. Eventually they will die from simple germs, and the true criminals never have to act upon them or deal with their resistance.

If you are old enough, you may remember a time when your throat wasn't sore all the time? Why is it that you think rates of Autism, Cancer, and Mental Illness, are climbing so. How much longer will you wait? How much sicker do they need to make you, before you believe that this is real? How long before you stand up for yourself, and stand up for your children?

I do not know when that point comes that it is too late to fight back. It may already be. I know, for myself it may be too late. The stress of living, and living in a poisoned environment over came me eventually. During a financial crisis I developed Ramsey Hunt Syndrome, which is a form of Bells Palsy . It is said that certain vaccines (which I had been exposed to in childhood) were engineered to cause auto immune problems later in life when triggered by stress.

Bells Palsy has been linked to vaccines. In my case, the Ramsey Hunt Syndrome is said to be caused by dormant chicken pox virus that laid quietly in my cell, since my childhood vaccination, and was reactivated by stress. Overnight I lost use of the left side of my face, because the facial nerve gets attacked and basically dies. A new one must grow back eventually in its place.

In my case it's been with mixed success.

While being treated for that, they found I had a meniginoma, which is a small brain tumor. We are not sure how long it was there, but for now it is small enough that we are just watching it. Watching and waiting to see if a brain tumor grows has been a unique journey. While it is stressful, it is also an opportunity to come face to face with my fears. In my case, it has helped me to find more courage to say the things in my book and on my blogs that I now say.

I am living proof that it is not hard, in today's world, to worry yourself sick. Economic oppression, psychological anxiety, and biological warfare, has left me with physical reminders of just how real the agenda of the globalists can be. It has also let me show with my life, and work, that you can rise above any circumstance, and move in a positive direction!

For if I am able to come from where I came from, and go through everything that I have been through, so can you! We can be, do, or have anything in life that we can conceive of. I believe we each where born at this time for a reason. Have you found your reason yet? Have you tasted your passion? We need to drop fear, and pick up love! Fear is not real. It is only a decision!

Resist the tyranny of the elite

"The tree of liberty must be refreshed from time to time with the blood of patriots and tyrants"
- Thomas Jefferson

I will not pretend to fool myself, nor any of you, and say that it will be easy to defeat the international bankers. They have the money, the resources, and the organization in place. I want you to understand that times will get tougher before they get better. The price of this victory will be very high. It may cost you all you presently hold dear, even your very life.

You must be prepared to defend your home, yet you also must prepare to leave it. You must be prepared to fight for your employment. You must be prepared to sacrifice for it, yet you also must be prepared if it is no longer available.

I do not say that lightly, in fact, I wish I did not even have to go there, but the banksters have corrupted the government, and through the government they have erected structures to contain, control, and eliminate people that they will label domestic terrorists (mainly, people who oppose them). Through FEMA and Homeland Security they have been silently erecting thousands of detention centers. I recommend you go on the internet and see them for yourself. I have several such videos on my website (see back pages).

They say they are for terrorist attacks, but they built mass detention centers, connected them to railways, lined up millions of plastic coffins, mass graves, and built some of these facilities with gas furnaces too large to be just for heating. After reading this book, do you really trust them? I do not. I also know that the Bush family helped fund Hitler and his efforts, and I know that similar facilities were built back then. I imagine that the people back then use to think that no government could be so evil as to actually build human furnaces and the like, and that they would never find people to participate in such crazy talk.

It is clear to me what their intentions are, and I know that any fight begun now, will most likely not end in my lifetime. What we are looking at will be more like a hundred year struggle, similar to the Muslim's intifada. So prepare, and remember in the immortal words of John Lennon, "war is over, if you want it".

For the banksters lose the moment you stop giving them power over your mind. One by one we can awaken and claim our independence. As you wake up, try to share this information with others. Some will welcome the information, others will try desperately to cling to the old myths they were taught. Your only task is to maintain your light. You are not responsible for anyone else's light.

Non Cooperation is our key weapon. The more people that stop cooperating with the machine the quicker we can clog its gears. Give your heart and mind to the effort. Throw your body into the gears and bring it to a grinding halt!

I know that this book may very well be the death of me. I have made peace with the possibility that it may lead to my imprisonment. I want to state publically that I hold no ill will against anyone in the government, nor in the banking establishment.

The following is from the last speech Martin Luther King Jr. gave, the night before he was assassinated:

"But I know, somehow, that only when it is dark enough, can you see the stars. And I see God working in this period of the twentieth century in a away that men, in some strange way, are responding — something is happening in our world. The masses of people are rising up. And wherever they are assembled today, whether they are in Johannesburg, South Africa; Nairobi, Kenya; Accra, Ghana; New York City; Atlanta, Georgia; Jackson, Mississippi; or Memphis, Tennessee — the cry is always the same — "We want to be free."

And another reason that I'm happy to live in this period is that we have been forced to a point where we're going to have to grapple with the problems that men have been trying to grapple with through history, but the demand didn't force them to do it. Survival demands that we grapple with them. Men, for years now, have been talking about war and peace. But now, no longer can they just talk about it. It is no longer a choice between violence and nonviolence in this world; it's nonviolence or nonexistence.

That is where we are today. And also in the human rights revolution, if something isn't done, and in a hurry, to bring the colored peoples of the world out of their long years of poverty, their long years of hurt and neglect, the whole world is doomed....

Well, I don't know what will happen now. We've got some difficult days ahead. But it doesn't matter with me now. Because I've been to the mountaintop. And I don't mind. Like anybody, I would like to live a long life. Longevity has its place. But I'm not concerned about that now. I just want to do God's will. And He's allowed me to go up to the mountain. And I've looked over. And I've seen the promised land. I may not get there with you. But I want you to know tonight, that we, as a people, will get to the promised land. And I'm happy, tonight. I'm not worried about anything. I'm not fearing any man. Mine eyes have seen the glory of the coming of the Lord"...

Longevity does have it's place, but I submit to you that living a moment in true light is worth it. Like Jesus, when we throw the money changers out and disrupt their way of doing business they will seek to crucify us. They will prepare crosses and seek to nail us to it. We must be prepared for that day, and that possibility.

There are many ways to resist tyranny. It is not as important which you do, as much as it is the fact that you consciously choose to do something. We will all be called on to help in this struggle. Not just for your personal freedom, but for all your fellow human beings, and the planet as a whole.

There are direct actions you can take, if that is your inclination. You can join a protest group, sign petitions, or be part of an Abundance Group, for example. You can choose to write, or post articles and videos about what you believe (on the internet, or underground if need be), and what you see going on. Some may be attracted to financial protests or acts of non cooperation.

The New World Oder is so vast, that we will need your individual expertise and abilities to hit them back on as many fronts as possible. Your skills as a teacher, carpenter, businesswoman, or office worker; are all equally needed. Share this information with as many people as possible. Some people will awaken, and some may fear the information. Be patient, and persist.

There are many countries around the world that sponsor tyranny. Some times against their own citizens as in Russia, with the KGB, or England with the MI5. In the United States we have multiple agencies like the CIA, NSA, and Homeland Security. These agencies that on the surface supposedly strive to keep it's citizen's safe from outside threats instead are used to suppress their own citizens from various forms of redress against their governments.

Israel has a different strategy. I have a Jewish background. My mother was Jewish and I grew up being taught to have unquestioning faith in Israel. In fact any one who questioned Israel would come under immediate chastisement by other Jewish people in particular. This would happen not only at my family dinner table, but I was once even called in to speak to the chairman of my psychology department at college, who was Jewish, and asked about why I, a Jew, was writing against Israel (and that was back in the 1980's) in my newspaper column.

As I became more politically aware, however I learned of more and more about Israel's true strategy, not only around the world, but inside the United States. I learned it is called Zionism. You can be Jewish and not be Zionist. You can even be an Israeli, and not be Zionist. Zionism is the belief that Jewish people alone have a God given right to the land in Palestine. It is a political and religious ideology.

Zionists believe that any action is justified in the name of Zionism, whether the act is defensive or offensive. Like George W. Bush believed in America's right to preemptive strikes, Zionists believe that Israel can act preemptively and covertly. Quite a few of the top US administration positions, certainly since President Reagan, are held by people with "dual Israeli and American citizenships". Not by mistake, you also find that many of these same people have key roles in the World Bank, IMF, UN, CFR, Bilderberg, Trilateral Commission, Club of Rome. In effect they are making worldwide policy decisions, and have a major seat at the top of the NWO pyramid.

Thus decisions favorable to Israel can get carried out on a worldwide basis. Whether it is to level UN sanctions against Iran, or for President Obama to send another 30,000 troops into Iraq.

This is not so say that Israel is the only country to try and influence

other countries, but they are the most influential. Not just because

they get billions of dollars in aid, but because they can bring to the

government of Israel TRILLIONS worth of influence!

Educate yourself and others

The amount of information you will be required to take in

over the course of your awakening is vast. There are multiple

sources for gaining insight and understanding of what has

happened, and what is yet to happen. There are also proven

strategies that you can learn to employ to defeat the agenda against

you. At the end of this book will be a list of websites that you can

go to get educated about all the things I touch on in this book.

The plot against you is intricate and on one hand has taken

many generations to shape. While on the other hand, it is

amazingly simple. The plot as I see it, consists of 4 stages. The key

to understanding how the elite think is to remember the phrase they

are most famous for: "competition is sin". Today, the only

competition for a World Government would be The United States. We are the only super power left. Thus, before they are able to establish a world government and have it truly be unstoppable, they need to eliminate the power and influence of the United States, and its people. Otherwise, there could be an uprising, and a true leader might be elected who would then command an army, that not only has nuclear weapons, awesome fire power, but also bases in a hundred plus countries around the world.

The elite can not take that chance. The threat needs to be eliminated. This is how I believe they will plan to do it:

The Elite's Plan For World Domination

1. Kill The Dollar

Through their corporate state they can use corporations like Goldman Sachs (which they own) to manipulate, oil prices, and financial instruments, like derivatives. Through the Federal Reserve Bank (which they own) they can manipulate complex bailouts that promise one thing, but deliver another. Wealth can be redistributed, and the dollar collapsed. The Media (which they own) can be used to keep the people confused and misdirected. Bailouts and wars can plunder the economy and the dollar. Eventually the bubble will burst and the dollar will collapse.

2. Bring The United States To Third World Status

As I stated above, the elite cannot allow a powerful United States to exist. They must weaken it to the point that it is no longer a threat. When people are so busy just trying to survive, they do not have the time, or ability to oppose you. The elite have historically used a trickle up, pyramid, model. Through taxes, fees, fines, and the things you need for daily living that you purchase through their corporations, the majority of your money will trickle up to them. They will seek to return the world to a two class society. The very rich elite, and the very poor masses.

3. Use Reform Acts To Bring In Complete Government Control

They will try to set up a complete Tax and Control Grid over the American people (and the world). Through a series of legislative acts they will take control of healthcare, food, internet…etc. Under the guise of regulation, they will self administer fines, taxes, and the out right ability to shut down anything, and anyone who they feel like. They will be judge, jury, and executioner.

Hidden inside the fine print of the over 2,500 page Healthcare bill is the authority for government, through the IRS (which they own) to collect healthcare taxes, fees, and penalties, through direct withdrawal , seizure, or garnishment of your paycheck and bank account. If that is not enough they will hold over your head the threat of imprisonment, or the elimination of your ability to buy, sell, drive, travel or receive healthcare.

4. Instituting Themselves As Head Of a One World Government

Once the obstacles are out of the way, like the American people, and the control grid is laid down around the world, they will bring in a One World Government. It will not be like anything we have now, but probably mostly resembling China. China is almost already there, so the amount of upheaval will be less there than in the west. Although westerners will have to change the most, poor people all around the world will suffer the greatest.

Escape the matrix you were born into

In the movie, The Matrix, the main character, Neo has his adventure only begin when he is awaken from the Matrix, and sees for a fact that he had been hooked up to it. Likewise, your escape has only begun, because you now have the knowledge. The road in front of you is still long and hard, and riddled with danger.

Yes, the danger is real, and will become more real, as the corporate government begins to crack down on the people who are waking up. Do not fool yourself. They have been planning for the people inevitably waking up. They have prepared the law to favor them and their agenda for control. The facilities to detain you are up and ready, and their slaughter mechanisms are awaiting the push of a button.

That is why it is important that you understand how much you have to be committed to this, and how much you have to be willing to sacrifice when the time comes. Few revolutions are bloodless, and this being the granddaddy of them all, I suspect it will get quite messy.

I am not saying that you should march yourself into the gas chambers, but I am saying that you should be prepared for a long and hard fight, and one that may require you giving up all that you hold dear. Your family, your loved ones. To save them, you must be prepared to be separated from them. You will need to become secure in your being able to be alone, or they will use that to subjugate your cooperation with the system.

Detaching from the matrix will be different for each person. We are all hooked in differently and to different degrees, so unhooking from it must also be different for each person. I will discuss the major ways you can detach from the matrix, but I am by no means saying it is the only right way for everyone.

Kill your TV set, or at least begin to withdraw from it. As you awaken you will see how the media is riddled with propaganda. In fact TV is now completely a propaganda tool of the corporate state. The majority of stations are owned by corporations owned by just a small handful of men. Political parties, and government agencies use the media to shape public opinion. Not to report on it anymore.

Be more careful what food you buy. Support companies who use non GMO and non irradiated foods. Support the opposition to implementation of Codex Alimentarius. This is an international effort run through the United Nations, which has been slowly, over the last several decades been trying to change countries food regulations to support GMO grown food over natural foods, and vitamin supplements. Spearheaded by big money corporations, like Monsanto they seek to regulate smaller companies and individual farms out of existence. They have been successful in many countries around the world and soon similar regulations making non GMO foods (natural) illegal are likely to go into effect here.

The time to speak up and voice your opposition is now. You need to let your representatives know that you do not want them voting for anything that contains Codex Alimentarius regulations. Let your friends know too, and check the food that you buy to see whether it is being made with GMO seeds. You will be surprised at just how much of what most people eat has been genetically modified.

To make greater profits, companies are developing "terminator seeds" technology. Natural seeds yield a crop that grows back each year. A good farmer gets many good seasons out of a bag of seeds. A healthy crop will replenish itself. This however is not profitable to seed companies. Terminator seeds however, last only one season. Each year farmers will be forced to purchase new seeds. This drives up the price of farming, and the price you pay on the shelves. To those on the darkside, this is merely business.

The long term health effects of Codex Alimentarius, terminator seeds, and GMO's cannot be known. We do know however that cancer, autism, and neurological disease rates are rising. Time is running out, both in our outside world, and inside us.

Dr. Leonard Horowitz has devoted his life work to exposing that wall street bankers, population planners, and scientists, favorable to the globalist depopulation agenda, have been purposely infiltrated into every level of government, both here in the United States, and around the world. Toxins meant to dumb down, sterilize, and slow kill most of the world population, are being exposed to people, primarily through vaccinations.

Vaccine depopulation in the western world, works by destroying the immune system response slowly, over time. Live toxins, neurological agents, cancer causing chemicals, and adjuvants are mixed in with the supposed regular vaccine. An adjuvant (in theory) is a chemical agent that is added to a vaccine to strengthen the vaccine's potency against whatever the vaccine is protecting you from. Thus, if the vaccine is for something like the flu, the adjuvant is used to make it stronger at killing the flu virus. It can, however, have harmful effects on other cells in the body. Many adjuvants are known now to have carcinogenic, and neurological effects. The vaccine makers know this and still use them. Why? Because they want to depopulate you!

Some vaccine makers throw in high levels of adjuvants, or even live viruses and cancers. Some are from humans, and some are from animals. The effects are the same. A slow kill, and culling of the world's population, profitably. The sicker you become, the more drugs you have to buy.

Many of the biggest depopulationists sit on the boards of the drug companies, government agencies, the media, and financial institutions. They have even disguised philanthropic organizations to do the exact opposite of what the public thinks the organization is there for.

One such globalist is David Rockefeller. He is a well known philanthropist, and has been involved all his life with cancer "research". Yet, all his life, no cure for cancer can be found, or should I say, "allowed in". Instead the organizations become more about regulation and suppression of known cures. Treatments that citizens are not allowed access to unless they go outside of their country. Doctors are kept from doing the research they need to do, and some even lose their licenses or are jailed.

"We are grateful to The Washington Post, The New York Times, Time Magazine and other great publications whose directors have attended our meetings and respected their promises of discretion for almost forty years. It would have been impossible for us to develop our plan for the world if we had been subject to the bright lights of publicity during those years. But, the work is now much more sophisticated and prepared to march towards a world government. The supranational sovereignty of an intellectual elite and world bankers is surely preferable to the national auto determination practiced in past centuries."

- David Rockefeller, founder of the Trilateral Commission, in an address to a meeting of The Trilateral Commission, in June, 1991.

One of David Rockefellers organizations is Memorial Sloan

Kettering Cancer Hospital. While there are some fine doctors

there, and they have personally helped me, I know that in the

bigger picture there is a different purpose. Organizations like The

American Cancer Society is really meant to regulate and suppress a

cure. Planed Parenthood, another Rockefeller organization, is not

just for offering women choices, but instead it is to lower birth

rates. For example, because of organizations like this, 52% of

African Americans were never born. The founder of Planned

Parenthood, Margaret Sanger has said:

On African Americans, and immigrants:

*"...human weeds,' 'reckless breeders,' 'spawning... human beings
who never should have been born."*
    *- Margaret Sanger, Pivot of Civilization, referring to
immigrants and poor people*

On the extermination of African Americans:

*"We do not want word to go out that we want to exterminate the
Negro population," she said, "if it ever occurs to any of their more
rebellious members."*
*- Woman's Body, Woman's Right: A Social History of Birth
Control in America, by Linda Gordon*

My heart weeps when it thinks about the evilness of some of these people. They have plotted and schemed for hundreds of years. While the people toiled and slept, darkness grew up around them. As Wayne Dyer has said, this will be the first generation that will have a shorter life expectancy than their parents. This will also be a generation that will not make as much , per capita, as their parents did. They will have more toxins and releases of toxic chemicals, such as the oil spill in the Gulf o Mexico or depleted uranium used in bombs, bullets, and all the weapons we spread around the world.

The wide range of negativity available for the globalists to choose from can make you feel overwhelmed at times. Trying to protect yourself and your loved ones from everything can become a fulltime job in itself. Not knowing exactly what their next move is or where they are about to strike can be extremely stressful. Often, the more you awaken, the more this is so. Yet the choice to stay asleep is not a viable choice and will lead to much worse circumstances for yourself, and your loved ones.

A growing industry has risen up for people looking for various means of protecting themselves when that time becomes necessary. People will need to learn to "live off the grid". There are many good books, and videos that you can get to familiarize yourself with the choices available. The basic idea is prepare ahead of time. You will want to put together for your family a "Go Bag" or also called a "Boogie Bag". This is a bag that you can "grab" in and emergency and "go" immediately with.

1. Gold and silver coins, bars, or jewelry.
2. Water and water filter / purifier.
3. Storable food.
4. Seeds / Garden
5. A means of protection. (…ie guns, pepper spray…etc.)
6. Medicine

The list can be longer depending upon your location and needs. This is just a sample to get you started. You can do your own research and find many good suppliers. Many of these things are available on the internet.

Divest from the corporate state

Get out of the six largest banks. Try as best you can to not give money to large, international companies, and chain stores. Whenever possible, remember to shop, and spend your money locally, within your community. At this time in our history, it is also a good idea to get out of all paper money and most investments. Buying gold, if you can afford it, and silver, for the average person is a wise choice.

The road to independence will only come through sovereignty. The key to sovereignty is a concept called Allodial Title. Allodial Title means owning property free, clear, and completely.

Allodial Title is a very difficult thing to get in today's society since the people who run things are so aware of this. The Sovereignty Movement, and becoming a sovereign can be the next best thing. I have explained earlier in my book, that there is a UCC process for people who want to go that route. This is also difficult, and not for everyone's circumstances. The government also makes this process difficult, since they want to discourage it, and continue to profit from us.

So if you can't beat them, and you can't join them, what is a person to do? This is where an understanding of Liberation Psychology becomes so important. There is a third way. The Third Way involves changing your relationship with money, and the things money buys you. It involves divesting from the corporate state, and finding alternatives. Sometimes it will mean supporting alternative products, or sometimes it will mean learning to do without the thing altogether.

If you are lucky in life, you will find that money is not everything. Love, and freedom are more valuable than money. You might say "you can buy freedom", and you can to a degree, or at least the feeling of freedom. Real freedom however, is internal, not external. Someone cannot grant you freedom. They can free your body, but only you control the freedom of your mind.

Which is why your mind is so valuable. The corporate state knows this, and spends billions of dollars a year trying to control your mind. Not just through the media (which is completely corporate run at this point), but through chemicals in your water, like fluoride, and more and more advanced mind control technologies.

The only way to get free of the matrix is to unplug yourself. One plug at a time. Each time you find an alternative to purchasing from a large corporation, or doing without the item, you further unplug yourself. Some people run around totally free. Some are partially free, and that's ok, if that is working for them. It's not about right or wrong, or it being all good, or all bad. It's about what is the right level of being unplugged for each of us.

The key to remember when downsizing, or unplugging, is "smaller is better". Large companies are more likely tied into the corporate state. Presently the large companies have an agenda to do away with the smaller companies. The corporate state has bought off all 3 branches of government, and the media. The aim in the coming years will be for them to use regulation to make it unfeasible for small companies to survive, and have laws ready to remove them when they can't keep up.

By supporting small companies, and local establishments you not only keep them alive, but you will not be feeding the beast.

Without food the beast will die. At a campus sit in back in 1967 a

famous activist said:

*"There is a time when the operation of the machine becomes so
odious, makes you so sick at heart, that you can't take part; you
can't even passively take part, and you've got to put your bodies
upon the gears and upon the wheels, upon the levers, upon all the
apparatus, and you've got to make it stop. And you've got to
indicate to the people who run it, to the people who own it, that
unless you're free, the machine will be prevented from working at
all!"*   *- Mario Savio*

Overcome feeling helpless

As I have outlined for you in this book, the system that is

now in place is vast. I say to you however, that what is available to

you is even far vaster. Only a little bit of light is needed to

illuminate the darkest of spaces.

Once you have woken up, by reading books, like this,

watching videos, searching the internet, and talking to fellow

patriots, you have begun the first step. This waking up process

takes place on many levels, because you are beginning to see all the ways you have been misled, on each of these levels. This can be a time of feeling you are on an emotional rollercoaster. You are excited about everything you are learning, but also sad and even frightened by the darkness of what you are learning.

It's all necessary to your future growth. Some people may try and skip this step. They believe that by focusing only on positive thoughts they will attract more of the positive things in life. I understand that, however, you also leave yourself and your loved ones vulnerable to repeating the mistakes of the past.

I am writing this, because many of you (my friends) are noticing that times keep getting tougher and tougher. The daily assaults on our health, financial stability, and emotional ability to cope are increasingly more intense, or quickening. At the same time, your eyes are opening to the world around you. You are learning that you have been lied to, and worse yet, that the people who lied to you have been controlling the world, and are doing very bad things to you, that you feel powerless to stop.

You may have heard of the old science experiment called Pavlov's Dog. In it a dog is put into a cage like maze, and fed each time a light goes on. Eventually the dog learns that when the light comes on it's going to be time to eat. They found that the mere fact of the light coming on makes the dog begin to salivate. What later experiments found however was that if the dog was inconsistently rewarded with food, or not at all, then the light coming on would lose its effect. Eventually the dog learns helplessness and begins to just lay there, never even searching for the food when the light comes on.

We have become like those dogs. Feeling helplessness at the state of our world, and our lives. You are trying to maintain a positive attitude on the inside, while all around you your world is crashing down around you? There IS a reason that this generation is the first generation, in recent memory, that will have less than the previous one. The truth is you have been lied to, manipulated, and set up, your entire life. The game was set up way before you were even born. Your parents were lied to also, and their parents before them.

While they toiled under these lies, it is only now, in this generation, that ignorance of this system will lead to total disaster. For the power elite that run the game are calling in their cards. This is the pivotal point in history that everything can change. You must wake up. You can regain your vision by learning how to see around their lies. You can be free from those who seek to control you!

Why resist???? If the above isn't reason enough to want to resist what is coming, there are other reasons too. I see the answer to that existing on 4 levels. There has been a cabal of European men that began several centuries ago to organize and amass great power. Eventually people from other countries like the United States joined this cabal of what became international banking families. Their wealth grew so large that they began financing countries, and indebting them, through causing wars. The people of the countries involved with the wars would have to give larger and larger percentages of their labor and wealth to the bankers to pay off the debt on the money the country borrowed.

Today, the banking families own everything, including the media, which they use to promote THEIR own interest. They own the government. I mean, literally own the government. Congress gave all our land to them in 1871, and then sold each citizen and our labor in 1913 with the Federal Reserve banking System, and then again in 1932 by assigning us birth certificates, in exchange for loans, trying to get us out of the Great Depression (which of course the bankers caused).

It would be easy to close your eyes, and let the banksters continue to take everything you have. The price for that, however, is too high. I will outline the 4 reasons you MUST resist:

Physical Reasons:

1. Their agenda includes eliminating you, your children, and everyone you love. It is called Agenda 21. It was written by the banksters, and their henchmen, we will call "globalists". They are preparing for one word government, controlled by, guess who....them! To do this they say they must eliminate the world's population down to a controllable size for the banking families to control. They published that this was about 500 Million. Which means 90% of us (6.5 billion people) have to be eliminated. They call it the Great Culling. They are poisoning us slowly through the air we breathe, water we drink, and food we eat. By causing cancer and autoimmune disease they are trying to out and out kill us, and sterilize us so that our population growth dwindles, to the point that it reverses, and we begin to depopulate. This is all

documented. They have written down everything they plan to do to us. Just google "Agenda 21".

2. They are making you Debt Slaves. Slavery did not end after the civil war. Nor did the king leave after we won our "so called" independence in 1776. They change the name, but not the game. The British Empire, through the Rothschilds, and banking families continued to buy and influence politicians to approve loans through them, and before long got the lawmakers to give them title to the land that our forefathers fought and died for. Through the Federal Reserve (owned by the European banking families), and the IRS (owned by the European banking families) we are completely manipulated into them controlling the money supply, taxation, and our very freedom. As we increasingly work, if they let us, more and more for them, and less and less for ourselves, and families.

Mental Reasons

There are mental reasons to resist. The New World Order, that the globalists are creating has one main aim. That is to control your mind. Through slight of hand, and distraction they are trying to manipulate you to participate in your own destruction....and pay them, while you do it!

Fluoride in the water, for example is a known neurotoxin. It was also used by the Nazi's in the concentration camps, not just to kill the people, but to keep them calm, sedate, and dumb. Baruim is found being put in exhaust engines of planes, sometimes willingly, sometimes unwittingly, and being sprayed down on us for decades. It has no business being there, yet lab tests are showing it at toxic levels.

The main stream media, which is all owned by a handful of globalists will not tell you these things. There is a lot they won't tell you. Instead, what they will tell you is to BE AFRAID...and to beg your government leaders to regulate the big mega corporations (owned by the globalists), which ends up allowing them to pass laws that favor them.

They cause tragic events like 9/11, Middle East Wars, and The BP Disaster, not to mention Health Care Reform....and get you to accept greater and greater controls, and eliminations of your personal liberty, and finances. Always, when you follow the money, it leads up to them. The globalist, international banking families...

Emotional Reasons:

We need to come together emotionally. On a personal level, and on a planetary level. On a personal level we have to be honest with ourselves, and face up to the task in front of us. We have got to be willing to die on our feet, instead of our knees. You must resign yourself to a few facts:

1. This resistance struggle will be long.

2. You may not see the end of it in your lifetime (but perhaps your children will).

3. It will get worse, before it gets better.

Spiritual Reasons:

Spiritually, we need to understand a few things. By understanding these things it does not mean that we will not live through horror or experience tough times. It only means that we will experience it differently. From a place of LOVE and not FEAR. From an understanding that we are more than our bodies which are down here. We can act from the understanding that our struggle and resistance has meaning and benefit to not only us, but the world. Our energy is added on to the energy of the universe that is expanding and growing, even during the times it seems dark. Darkness is learning along with light, that only love is fruitful. All the other dark energies will eventually be shown to be useless, because in the end, only love can get us what we truly want.

Some may think they want riches, but what they really want is love. Some may think they want power, but what they really want is love. The so called "love" that may come with money and power eventually are seen as false, and the soul seeks out real love....and that love nourishes and expands....

Remember these 3 Principles:

1. You were born for this time.

2. You chose to come down here for this battle.

3. The transformation in you, that it will cause, will lead to your soul's growth.

Manifest your dreams and desires

Do you know why the caged bird sings? Even though it may be locked up it perceives itself free. Perception is all that is required. If you are free and sovereign on the inside, then no matter how many bars they place around you they cannot take your joy. Only you can give it away. Only you can decide to give it to them.

Anyone who survived a concentration camp knows this. Eli Weizel, Nobel Prize winner, has said, "I was born in a ghetto, but the ghetto was not in me". He means that he was born into a hard situation, poverty, discrimination...etc. Yet that is not what is inside him. Inside him was beauty, and hope, and dreams of a

273

better day. That day, finally came about, because he held tight to who he was inside, despite what his outer situation told him.

The key to being able to manifest your dreams and desires is the ability to FEEL the thing that you want to bring into your life, before it is actually there. You need to be able to FEEL AS IF you already are experiencing that which you want to bring into existence. If you do it good, your mind, and even your body, does not know the difference between the thought, and the actual thing.

Thought leads to feeling, which leads to vibration. Vibration is about frequency, and like any good radio, you can hone in on the frequency of the thing you want to be, do, or have. When you do it enough times there is little difference between you and the thing, and then it has become you, and you are what you were desiring.

Meditation and visualization are wonderful for achieving this. Picking a power spot to do your meditations and visualizations help magnetize your energy and your attraction ability. I use to have a favorite spot in nature, a tree that I would meditate under. While I was under this tree I would visualize what I wanted. I also used the tree to write poetry, and the words would come to me like I was channeling them.

My Poet Tree

There is a place I go
A place I know
Where I can get
A world away from me
Where brooks flow
Gently....

And time stops
Awhile
I loose a hundred years
And gain ten thousand

My poet tree finds me
I use to fool myself
And think it the other way around
Then one day while I was with my poet tree
A leaf glided down
And brushed my tears
Away....

And time stops
Awhile
I loose a hundred years
And gain ten thousand

My Poet Tree has been calling me
And I it
For so long
That when we are together again
We run to each other

My Poet Tree is a place
Where I can BE
Where I can SEE
Where I AM
And was ALWAYS
GOOD ENOUGH.....

~ Kazi Kearse

Chapter Seventeen

A New Normal

"It is not the strongest of the species that survive, nor the most intelligent, but the one most responsive to change."
~ by Charles Darwin

Why is it that we get sad, or mad…etc. I have shown you, in this book, that negative feelings come from negative thoughts. The key follow up question to that, however is where do negative thoughts come from? The answer is two fold. Remember, energy comes form thoughts. Negative energy may come from outside ourselves, or it may come from inside ourselves.

The negative energy that comes to us from outside ourselves can come from people, places, or things. An example could be corporate owned television that tries to disempower you, or make you think that some genetically altered food of theirs is good for you, when the exact opposite is true. There are millions of examples, but whenever anyone outside you tries to lower or take your energy, it is negative. This is true whether it's the TV, your neighbor, your preacher, spouse, or government.

We, however owe our success or failure equally to forces inside us. In fact as we progress in this game, the forces inside of us have even more power, and responsibility. I have spent thousands of hours counseling people, and I can tell you that how they feel depends on their thoughts, and their thoughts either are going in a negative direction, of lack, and hopelessness; or in a positive direction of hope, and feeling full.

Creating A New Normal is about learning to reinterpret old patterns of how we see our world. Far more than just "looking at our life through rose colored glasses", this is about physically creating changes within us chemically, and biologically; through thought, and also outside of us shaping our new landscapes, through vibration, and the law of attraction. This includes setting up our lives to be in vibrational match with the frequency of the thing we are trying to bring into our life. Like a radio, we must set our vibration to match the frequency we wish to pick up. So if you want "LOVE 105.5" you need to be tuned to that specific frequency, or it will pass your awareness, like the thousand other frequencies around you.

10 Spiritual Beliefs of Successful Creators

1. Form is an illusion. Everything in the universe, including yourself, is made up of energy. When energy vibrates it creates form. When the vibration changes, form changes.

2. You are an Eternal Being inside a human body at this moment.

3. Thoughts become things. Otherwise called "The Law Of Attraction", which basically says that what you are thinking about the most, will be drawn to you.

4. These "things" are really just lessons in disguise. These lessons do not end.

5. You are part of a loving, and expanding universe.

6. You are worthy of complete love.

7. This is an abundant universe.

8. Love and Well-Being are the dominant forces in the universe. Fear, and evil are not a forces, but merely the lack of Love and Well Being.

9.. There is nothing that must be done. Success or failure is merely a lesson. You understand that you do not finish, or truly complete anything in an expanding universe.

10. There is no beginning and there is no end.

If you should ever forget any or all of these beliefs, simply remember to be **JOYFUL**. For joy is the feeling state that all these beliefs are about getting to. To learn how to consciously express Joy was your main reason for coming into this existence.

Do not be afraid to dissent. I have learned the agony of fear well, and I have seen its false face. I know now that light is infinitely more powerful, and redemptive. As each human finds this out for themselves the light in the world will grow. Even as the times seem to grow darker and more difficult remember that you have an internal and eternal light. Even as you may find yourself surrounded by darkness, know that your own light can be maintained. You now know what they have tried so hard to hide from you.

There is a story about two mice that fell into a bucket of milk. They each tried to get out. As time went on they grew weary. One mouse said "it's useless to keep trying to get out. The walls are too high, and every time we try, we keep slipping and falling back down". That mouse drowned. The other mouse kept swimming. Slowly the milk began to spoil and thicken. Eventually it hardened into butter. The surviving mouse was able to leap out of the bucket!

Never give up. Never surrender. Your struggle now, will not only allow you to survive, but your children's children also. We can throw off these tyrants, but only if we keep our energies up, despite what our current circumstances may tell us. We have to see beyond it. Only by staying in the positive energy, and not cooperating with the thought system of needing to conform, will we guarantee victory one day.

Martin Luther King Jr. said that the moral arc of the universe is long, but it bends towards justice. I believe that. I believe it with my whole heart. I believe that when we all are able to remove fear as an obstacle, and have transcended it's legacy on our lives, we will each choose love. I feel that is true, not only for those of us securely on the path of light, but even for those still in darkness. There is one source, and that is light. Everything else is merely the degree of light given off, or the lack there of. I do not believe that there is a source of darkness. Even dark forces, I believe, are on a path, and will eventually choose love.

Love is the only choice. When fear is removed, or transcended, then we can see clearly. When we see clearly, we see that there really only was ever one choice. The choice to love. We can choose it now, or we can take another choice, like greed, or self doubt…etc, and eventually see that those choices end in pain, and dissatisfaction. When we choose love, however, if our mirror is wide enough, and our patience long enough, we find that it ends in joy and happiness.

That does not mean that you will not experience loss, or pain, it only means that you can transcend it. Once you transcend it, you can find a new normal. Throughout our lives we will need to find new normals. Nothing stays the same. Change is the great teacher in the universe. We need to see we are all pupils, and our classes never end.

We are never not in class. When we begin to see our difficulties as classes, we can see that there are bigger lessons we are experiencing. We can then have a different understanding of the loss, and pain we experience. We realize that they are not punishments for doing something wrong, by a wrathful God.

Diseases, like cancer, can be seen in a new perspective. You did not necessarily do anything wrong, or commit some transgression. When a lover leaves you, it is not because you are a bad person, or unlovable. There are reasons we may not see on the physical level. There are lessons, in classes, that our soul has signed up for that we cannot fully comprehend from this side.

Why would a soul sign up for a painful lesson? To understand that, we need to understand how a soul would see a particular physical incarnation. We must remember that we are eternal beings. Energy never dies. An eternal being knows that pain, and loss, are teachers, just like, love, and success, are also teachers.

Some teachers in school we liked more than others. Some were nicer to us, and others were very stern with us. We, however, learned from both of them. Some courses are harder than others, and require much more work. In fact, it often was the harder classes that we learned the most from.

It says in the bible, that in the end, "you reap what you sow". This is a universal law of the universe. When you "reap" something, you experience it, and you receive the results of what you were doing. When you "sow" something you are "taking an action", whether that is a physical action, mental, or spiritual action.

Change is another law of the universe, and it's benevolence acts on reaping, and sowing, and does something very important. It assures you that nothing you reap is permanent. So you are free to let go of fear.

You can have all the riches in the world but feel very unfulfilled. Yet if you have love and joy in your heart you do not need physical riches. This is one of the lessons a soul must learn in a lifetime. Your soul may be in this class right now, getting this particular lesson.

Do your lessons with love and joy and they will be much faster. That does not mean the class ends, simply because you do. Each soul knows exactly how long it needs to experience a lesson for. Your Ego needs to let go of needing to rush you through a lesson, or convince you, it's ok to skip it, or go around the lesson. Release your path to your soul. Your soul will guide you through your classes. Just like it's been doing since you were a spark of stardust.

There is great knowledge available from your soul. You should find a way to communicate with it regularly. Find something that you like to do such as meditation, walking, running, exercising, or even just sleeping, and asking your soul to use that time to teach you something. Your soul will respond to that invitation. You only need to open your being to hear it.

The Sky Is Falling, And It's A Good Thing

Do you remember the story of Chicken Little ? As a child it was my favorite story, and now I know why. It's a parable, that could be the key to aid us all in facing what is coming in the days ahead, and growing from it. I would like to share my insight with you...

Chicken Little was walking down the street one day, when an acorn fell from a tree and hit him in the head. A fox was watching him and was about to bounce on him when he noticed that other ducks and birds were coming around Chicken Little because he was getting them all worried about "the sky falling". He waited till there were many different birds around, but soon realized that he was greatly outnumbered. He needed to come up with a plan, so he dressed up like a policeman and told them he would save them if they just got into his police van.

Now, of course it wasn't a real police van. He just decorated it to look like one. He was really planning to lure them

284

on to the van and the drive them away and eat them. Once he got them all on the van he revealed to them the truth. That the sky is not falling, and that it was an acorn that fell from a tree. The fox laughed at the birds for being so gullible, and threw the acorn up into the air!

Just then Sergeant Hippo Heffty was flying by in a helicopter and the acorn got stuck in the copter gears! The helicopter crashed into the van with the birds in it, and they escaped to freedom!!!

How does this relate to our struggle today? Chemtrails cross our skies and literally do fall down on us. The New World Order, Agenda 21, and more lies than I can list, rain down on us on a daily basis. Economies around the world are collapsing and it appears there is no end in sight to the misery spreading around the globe. It is easy to think these are the end times

Like the fox, the greedy international banking families, lick their lips, as they spread fear around the globe. They realize though that there are many of us, and only a few of them, so they must come up with a sneaky plan. A plan where we destroy ourselves. Through a global ponzi scheme they can get us to drown ourselves in debt, until there is no other choice but to get on the van they drive up to load us into.

By believing their costumes, they get us to cooperate, and do the opposite of what is in our own interest. By believing in our higher selves / higher power we can crash and smash those vans before we ever have to get into them.

The truth can be revealed to us. The truth is, the sky is falling, but it's a good thing. No matter what happens we will learn lessons from it, find a way to survive, and be a better, more enlightened person because of it.

The Great Collapse Awakening

" Time evolves, and comes to a place where it renews again. There is first a purification time and then there is a renewal time. We are in the Time of Purification"
~ Red Crow

You can feel it in your bones can't you? Something is different. Something has changed. We've had down turns in the economy, and depressions before, but this is something more.

There has been some shift. We may not be able to verbalize it yet, but that doesn't mean that our bodies do not feel it.

We have two great opposing forces, never seen before on this planet occurring at the same exact time. On the one hand we have a deepening global great depression, which is in reality a dismantling, or collapsing in disguise. On the other hand, we have at the same time, a great awakening, not only politically, but of the entire human potential, emotionally, and spiritually. For the first time in history, humanity is waking up, in mass, to their enslavement by the international banking families. A monumental time in the history of mankind where fundamental choices of how we live will be made on both the international and individual level, by every single person. You will be forced to decide whether you will live in LOVE, or live in FEAR…????

Thus what we have occurring is an ongoing battle, or (at a deeper level) dance, between the forces of light and the forces of darkness. By your actions, or in actions, you will aid one of these forces. The forces of darkness hope you will choose to be silent. They hope to discourage you, or out right scare you into acquiescence. They make it fineable or even criminal to speak out against them.

The next two years are critical. Not just for us, but even for our children's children. You and I were born for this time, and for this struggle. It may get dark at times, and seem like all you have ahead of you is a life of misery, but maintain your focus and strength, and you will receive from it not just a victory of light over darkness, but on the personal level, a deep understanding of life, love, and humanity!

I could tell you what I think is going to happen, however the truth is I don't know. The outcome is dependent on YOU. How will you respond in this time of transition? Will you choose love or fear? Is the force of love strong inside you? I think it is. In fact I know that my words have been guided to you, because the universe knows that they will activate the force of love inside you. Rise up, this is the time that we were born for!!!

They Are Killing The World

The more I looked into the 3 largest disasters in history; I began to notice more and more things that they have in common with each other. If it is true, we must have the courage to uncover it and look it in the face, because if they've done these 3, they will no doubt do more. Light workers must become Light Bringers, bringing light into darkness, educating others, and transmuting the negative into positive energy.

I began by looking for commonalities between the 3 events. I noticed that there was only a short time between them. Here I was, alive for 49 years, yet nothing like this happened for 36 of them, and then suddenly 3 happen, one after the other.

The attacks of 9/11, the oil disaster in the Gulf of Mexico (on 4/20 – Hitler's birthday), and The earthquake in Japan (interestingly on 3/11) and resulting nuclear disaster, all had something in common. They were not just environmental disasters, but they were also economic disasters for the country that they took place in. An economic disaster designed to weaken the economy so that there is no other power around to challenge the New World Order (NWO). That is why after 9/11, an over a decade deepening recession / depression, and toxic spread of oil and corexit, and the countries in the middle east were sufficiently taken over; the NWO could set its sights on the next domino…Japan!

To the globalists, "competition is sin". Japan had one of the world's largest economies. As it did back in the 1940's when it was brought to it's knees by the international banking families latest technology, the atomic bomb. Today their weapon of choice was a weapon called HAARP. Although pushed publically as being used peacefully, it is owned by the Navy and is basically used as an earthquake machine and weather modifier.

Like they did in 9/11, and the BP oil rig, they sent an advance team out to prepare the site. In the case of Fukushima it was some "security renovations" along with bringing in Mox Fuel for the first time, just a few months before the earthquake would take place. Mox fuel is particularly many times more toxic and explosive. Scientist knew that if a large earthquake was caused, there would be a resultant tsunami that could be blamed for knocking out the power. If the back up safety mechanisms were disabled or didn't work, like in the World Trade Center, and on the BP oil rig, then the reactors would begin an unstoppable meltdown. Which is exactly what happened.

To do this the militaries of the United States and Israel reportedly developed a computer virus called Stuxnet. They used it to disable a nuclear facility that Iran was developing. Once it's begun it can send itself else where undetected. To other nuclear power plants, such as the one in Fukushima. That would ensure that full meltdowns would happen at all 6 reactors, and sad to say that is exactly what has now happened. And guess what? Stuxnet was found on 63 computers in Japan. Those are just the known cases.

One month before this, guess who was hired to install some security features in the Fukushima nuclear plant?...An Israeli security company!!! Remember who created the Stuxnet virus? I'm not surprised that none of the back up safety features worked at any of the 6 reactors. If this sounds familiar to 9/11, it should because remember who got put in to run "security" in the World Trade Center? George Bush's brother!!!...And remember who was working on the rig prior to the explosion?... Dick Cheney's company, Halliburton!!!

I've been studying the globalists for awhile now and I'm starting to notice certain patterns or tell tail signs that they are working behind the scenes. Something odd happens. After the disaster happens you expect the government leader to step out front and for the government to mount a massive response, but they never do. Took Bush awhile to get to ground zero, and then only for a photo op. Obama stepped back and let BP handle the oil clean up. Even when the government said no spraying of the toxic dispersant, corexit, BP just ignored them, and kept doing it their way. Which was to stay in line with the globalist's plan to spread the toxins. The government didn't stop them because they work for the same people...the international banking families.

When the reactors started melting down what did the Japanese leaders do? They stood back and let the company who owned them run the show. They even took it a step further and refused help.

Like in the Gulf they bumble around for a period of time. Try a little this here....and a little bit of that over there...and "oh no, nothings working".... And it goes on and on, as more and more toxins spread out... And they don't stop it until the globalists are good and ready. Then they suddenly "find" a solution.

So the question then is "what do we do about this"? The media won't tell you this but what has come out of Fukushima is equivalent to the fallout of hundreds of thousands of nuclear bombs. That means, in other words, that a nuclear war has just been launched on us. No rockets. No giant mushroom clouds wiping out cities. Just fallout. It's odorless, colorless, and soundless. Silently deadly it comes down in the rain, blows in the winds, and jet streams, or travels in the ocean currents. Through a process called bio accumulation the radio active particles slowly accumulate inside every living thing it comes into contact with.

Unless we find a cure for cancer, or nuclear fallout, the eugenicists and their dream of depopulation that they've begun may very well wipeout most of the planet... But not if I have anything to do with it! Their goal of witling us from almost 7 billion people down to 500 million has begun, but will fail. We will come together and share information. Together we are capable of finding a way out of this mess!

The globalists and government officials have prepared underground structures for themselves. Some as large as small cities with miles of tunnels. They have stored up grains and seeds of all types to re grow things after the "culling" or "thinning" as they call it. I don't know how they plan to do this, but just because it's crazy, doesn't stop these psychopaths from trying it.

I've heard that most people who get sick from the radiation will take 2 – 15 years before the damage overwhelms them. I believe that the strong, the smart, and the lucky, can survive this. Here are some suggestions I've come across:

1. Potassium Iodide

2. Vitamin D3

3. Chlorella

4. Kelp

There are many others. The key will be to keep your immune system as strong as possible. We all have cancer cells and various toxic particles, including background radiation, inside our body all the time. Our immune system fights them off if the amount is not too high, and if our immune system is active.

I'm not telling you all this to scare you, or be dramatic. In fact I hope that the experts that I researched this information from are wrong…. But if they are even half right, we need to take action right now. For my kids, I want them to know that daddy tried to do something. I don't know why we were born at this time… But I know we were born for this time….

Rage, rage, rage against the dying of the light…!!!!!!

Our Time of Transition Has Begun

I'm torn whether I should give you the good news or the bad news first, because what I am about to tell you will contain both. You got up this morning, and went about your day as usual, and you might not even have noticed it, unless you stop, and look closely at things around you. Through incrementalism, those in power have been working behind the scene, to change your world, and tighten their control over you and the resources in your world. In short to enslave you.

The changes have been made gradually over generations, but are quickening now. Days, weeks, months, years, fly bye now. We talk among each other how time has sped up, and its true. We know it.

I take some solace in the fact that this time has been predicted. The forces that are taking down our world, actually are playing a role in the grander scheme of things, and are actually making way for a new world, and a new human. In fact we were born at this time because our souls wanted to be here to take part in the evolution.

How we will work, go to school, raise a family...etc., in the midst of this transition, I do not know. Yet, I know we will need to do it with love. For only the love vibration can protect us, and only in the love vibration can we see who is not working with us, and who in fact is working against our interests.

By taking a close look at the world around us, and connecting the dots, we can decipher the workings of a dark cabal of international banking families. They are power hungry. They have all the money in the world (almost literally), and do not want for anything, except more power. Power over their last plaything, YOU...

"The word justice is being misspelled. It's J-U-S-T – U-S. The white-shoe boys, as I call them, there's no justice for them. Like this guy, Corzine. 'I can't find 1.2 billion dollars'? Who can get

away with that crap? You see him at these hearings with the other

flunkies asking him questions. Did you see the plaque in front of

his name? "The Honorable Jon Corzine." Honorable, my ass!

Who's the head of the regulatory agency CFTC, Gary Gensler?

He was one of the lieutenants for Jon 'the Don' Corzine when

Corzine was head of the Goldman Sachs gang, before he became

senator of New Jersey. You get it?

Who's Obama's Chief of Staff? Bill Daley, from that wonderful

Daley machine in Chicago. Where did he come from? Oh, vice

chairman of Morgan Chase. Who was Bush's treasury secretary?

Oh, Henry 'Frankenstein' Paulson. Where was he from? He began

as the CEO of Goldman Sachs after Jon 'the Don' Corzine left.

This is the guy who created TAARP and came up with the BS line

of 'too big to fail.' Him? Yeah, that's right.

And who's the guy under Clinton that was treasury secretary who

put into process the deregulation of the financial industry and the

ultimate killing of the Glass-Steagall Act, which prevented

commercial banks becoming investment banks? Investment banks!

What a bunch of baloney that is. Casinos that gamble, and we have

to pay them now when they make bad bets. That couldn't be Robert

Rubin, could it, the former co-chair of Goldman Sachs? And who's

the guy now that they just put on the head of the European Central

Bank, Mario Draghi? Where was he from? Didn't he run the

European division of Goldman Sachs? And wait a minute now ...

what's this guy in Italy now, Mario 'Three-card Monte'? Wasn't he

an international advisor for Goldman Sachs?"

-Rant from Gerald Celente in 2013

The moneychangers are taking over the temple; you don't

have to go very far to look. It's right there in front of everybody's

eyes and no one will call a spade a spade. The first banksters

would be jealous to see what the Goldman Sachs gang, the JP

Morgan Chase criminal operation, the Citigroup crooks, the

Deutsche Bank bandits and the rest have pulled off.

I believe that we have to watch out for something along the

lines of economic martial law. The European system is in collapse.

The financial system in the United States is just as tenuous, if not

more, and I believe they will not admit there will be a financial

crash but rather they will use a geo-political issue to get the people

in a state of fear and hysteria whereby they'll then call a bank holiday or devaluation of the currency, or a hyperinflation of the currency, and blame it on somebody else. Right now the prime scapegoat seems to be Iran., but the true aim is to bring in a world wide currenecy.

The United States and the European Union have declared war on Iran. Let's call it what it is. They are making it impossible for Iran to sell oil. It's a form of warfare. Just as history has been re-engineered as with WWII, when you look back, it's a reverse situation of what the Americans did to the Japanese by cutting them off from oil. Now they are cutting the Iranians off from selling oil. Oil accounts for more than half of their GDP. They're the third largest oil supplier in the world. And US senators in Washington voted a hundred to zero to impose sanctions on Iran in the Senate. So I believe that Iran is going to be the flashpoint war that's going to be used as the cause to call martial law – economic martial law. And now, of course, that Obama has signed it into law on December 31 – Happy New Year, everyone – the National Defense Authorization Act will have the military in place to take care of any *"belligerent"* out there!

A leaked memo about Greece distributed to senior officials in Europe, lays out the truth. It warned that two of the new bailout's main principles might be self-defeating. Forcing austerity on Greece could cause debt levels to rise by severely weakening the economy while its €200bn debt restructuring could prevent Greece from ever returning to the financial markets by scaring off future private investors. "Prolonged financial support on appropriate terms by the official sector may be necessary," the report said.

In other words: These so called bailouts were never expected to really work, and are just meant to make the country, and it's citizens in prolonged debt to the international banks at high interest rates, which puts you in debt slavery!

What if Greece or any of the countries just refuse to pay? The bankers still come out ahead, because they can just crash any or all economies around the world, survive it on their private islands, or underground bunker, and buy everything up on the cheap!

So the elite are stocking up, buying record amounts of bullets, bread, and building underground shelters. They have privatized the space program and will soon be flying (rich) citizens into space. They are preparing to survive a period of cataclysm. A period of time between the collapse of our known society, around the world, and the beginning of their New World Order.

The memo that they are not giving you however, is that they don't include YOU in their future plans. Through famine, disease, and war, they plan to "cull" us to a much more sustainable number of slaves, Eventually they will not even need humans because robots will be everywhere. In fact, ultimately they plan to merge with robots and travel to other planets...

I have prepared you well for what is ahead. We have looked under every rock together. You now know how the world works, and you have the tools you need to go forth and change the world. Join with others and break the grip the dark cabal has over the world. You reading this book is not by chance, it was destiny! I love you very much...

"Love is everywhere, if we see it, and nowhere if we don't"
                                                        - Kazi Kearse

And So This Book Will End

And so this book will end for now, as all things must. Still we know now that even this book is energy, and will never die, but will live on in the hearts and minds of those it touches. I had several aims in writing this book, and I hope I have achieved them all. I wanted to help others along the way, and share the insights I have been lead to. I also, hope I have left a marked trail, so that any seeker, or truth teller, may be spared the mistakes I made.

We know that all endings are new beginnings, and so it is with these words. For my wantings will spawn wantings to sprout from your heart. Once even a pebble is thrown in a lake, the ripples spread out and the lake will never be quite the same lake again. Always remember that the caterpillar thought it's world was over, and then it became a BUTTERFLY !!!!!

I would like to end with the words of a man who originally "woke me up", Ram Dass:

"You are loved just for being who you are, just for existing. You don't have to do anything to earn it. Your shortcomings, your lack of self-esteem, physical perfection, or social and economic success— none of that matters. No one can take this love away from you, and it will always be here."

The New World Order can try and take away your freedom, your health, your money, and your family, but the one thing they cannot take is your LOVE...

Invictus

by William E. Henly

Out of the night that covers me,
black as the pit from pole to pole,
I thank whatever gods may be,
for my unconquerable soul.

In the fell clutch of circumstance,
I have not winced nor cried aloud,
under the bludgeonings of chance,
my head is bloodied but unbowed.

Beyond this place of wrath and tears,
looms but the horror of the shade,
and yet the coming of the years,
finds, and shall find me, unafraid.

It matters not how straight the gate,
how charred with punishment the scroll,
I am the master of my fate,
I am the captain of my soul.

There is a Breeze Blowing

There is a breeze blowing
I cannot deny it any longer
First it was a gentle nudging
But that swirl is now a mighty wind
That will uproot all that I know
All that I planted and watched grow
Is carried up to God

God laughs at our plans
Especially the well thought out ones
Nature knows the truth
Implanted in every blade of grass
Our cars, our phones,
Our lovers, our homes
They do not last

I want what lasts after the storm
What was there before, and evermore
I stand and await the rainbow
That lays hidden behind the clouds
Dormant inside us all

This time when the lightening bolt of love passes me
I will grab it, and take it deep inside
Yes....Yes there is a breeze blowing!

- Kazi Kearse

Online Site:
www.kazikearse.com

- **Sign up for counseling and mentoring**

- **Purchase from Product Store**

- **Sign up for membership and email list.**

- **Read Kazi's Blog**
  http://kazikearse.blogspot.com

- **Video Reference Library**
  www.youtube.com/changecomin